Advance Prais

NAVIGATING THE ROUGH WATERS OF TODAY'S PUBLISHING WORLD

"Confused by the ever-changing publishing landscape? Marcia Meier shows you the way. Tapping into her extensive industry contacts, she brings you the best thinking on where books and publishing are headed in the coming years. *Navigating* is an indispensable resource that should be on every writer's bookshelf."

—Arianna Huffington, author and founder
of *The Huffington Post*

"As the former director of one of the nation's most prestigious writers conferences, Marcia Meier knows what's happening in the book world. In *Navigating*, she brings her considerable writing skills and her connections together to help writers make sense of publishing trends today."

—Catherine Ryan Hyde, author of *Pay It Forward*
and *Becoming Chloe*

NAVIGATING THE ROUGH WATERS OF TODAY'S PUBLISHING WORLD

Critical Advice for Writers from Industry Insiders

by Marcia Meier

Fresno, California

Navigating the Rough Waters of Today's Publishing World

Published by Quill Driver Books,
an imprint of Linden Publishing
2006 South Mary, Fresno, California 93721
559-233-6633 / 800-345-4447
QuillDriverBooks.com

Quill Driver Books and Colophon are trademarks of
Linden Publishing, Inc.

ISBN 978-1-884995-58-3

135798642

Printed in the United States of America
on acid-free paper.

Library of Congress Cataloging-in-Publication Data

Meier, Marcia.
  Navigating the rough waters of today's publishing world : critical
advice for writers from industry insiders / by Marcia Meier.
      p. cm.
  Includes index.
  ISBN 978-1-884995-58-3 (pbk. : alk. paper)
  1. Authorship--Marketing. 2. Authors and publishers. I. Title.
  PN161.M455 2010
  070.5'2--dc22
                            2010010126

Contents

In memory of my dad and mom, Robert B. and Helen J. "Pat" Meier. I miss them every day.

Acknowledgments

Writing a book is a huge undertaking, and I am indebted to many people who helped in some way, either by reading the manuscript for content and typos, by opening up space for me to work on it, or by offering to get me out of my office and into the sunshine for a much-deserved break.

First, I am very grateful to the many editors, agents, and authors who contributed to this book in some fashion. Their expertise and wisdom were a tremendous help to me as I formed my own thoughts on the current trends in publishing. And their varied experiences added interest and provided examples that shine throughout the book.

I want to acknowledge a number of people for their help and encouragement throughout the process of writing. First, thank you to Kendall, my amazing daughter, who (mostly) allowed me the time to devote to this project. Thanks to Fred Klein, retired vice president and marketing executive with Bantam Books and a dear friend, who read the manuscript and provided valuable suggestions and improvements. Thanks to my writing buddies, The Pudding-line, for years of inspiration and for helping me stage an amazing conference every year: Grace Rachow, Jim Alexander, Ernie Witham, Toni Lorien, Linda Stewart-Oaten, Susan Chiavelli, Susan Gulbransen, Bob and Cathy DeLaurentis, Karl Bradford, Lucy Llewellyn Byard (our Sri Lanka connection), Julia Dawson,

Steven Anders, Ned Bixby, Bradley Miles, Steve Beisner, and Melinda Palacio. Thanks to Diana Raab for her unwavering support and friendship, and thanks to all my girlfriends, particularly Cathy Armstrong, Wendy Rockwood, Joan Bolton, and Linda Branch (the best conference ombudswoman ever), who called with invitations to walk on the beach, see a movie or go to lunch when I most needed them. Thanks to my book club gals, who were my Friday night escape every six weeks and who supported me through ups and downs: You're the best! Thanks also to photographers Mark Bennington and Robert DeLaurentis for their generosity. And, finally, to Steve Mettee, Kent Sorsky, and all the folks at Quill Driver Books, who went above and beyond to help me create this book—thank you!

Introduction: Comes the Revolution

"An incurable itch for scribbling takes possession of many, and grows inveterate in their insane breasts."—Juvenal, Satires

The publishing world is in the throes of a great upheaval. The global economic earthquake that began in 2008 shook many businesses at their core and accelerated changes that were already convulsing the publishing industry. Traditions that served for nearly one hundred years were replaced with new processes driven by emerging technology. Venerable publishing houses cut back on title releases or merged with one another in an effort to survive. By the end of 2009, the Association of American Publishers reported that year-to-date hardcover sales were up a modest 6.9 percent after two years of declining sales, although adult paperback sales were down by 5.2 percent for the year and the adult mass market category was down 4 percent. One other small bright spot was an increase of 2.2 percent in the year's sales of children's/young adult hardcover books.

On the other hand, bookstores reported an annual decline in 2009 of 1.8 percent in sales of new books, to $16.6 billion, the lowest level since 2003, according to the Census Bureau. Bookstore chains continued to struggle, and some of the nation's most famous independent bookstores—including Dutton's in Brentwood and Stacey's in San Francisco—closed their doors. Layoffs, closures, and mergers increased worries among writers and, indeed, everyone involved in book publishing.

Newspapers were also in distress. For all their efforts during the past fifteen years, newspaper publishers still haven't figured out how to make money on the Internet. As the economic crisis deepened, a number of major newspapers folded, throwing journalists into the ranks of writers looking for work.

The state of flux isn't expected to end anytime soon. This truly is a revolution, driven by technological change and an emerging publishing milieu akin to the old Wild West. Anything goes. Or, at least, anything seems possible. Who could have imagined, even two years ago, that an Internet-based Web site that invites people to share their opinions—*The Huffington Post*—would become what many believe may be a new model for journalism? The brainchild of Arianna Huffington, the site initially was one big blog. The well-connected Huffington invited all of her friends and acquaintances (including this author) to share their thoughts for free on *The Huffington Post*, and it has since grown into a major player in the world of policy, politics, and journalism. In early 2009, *The Huffington Post* announced it would venture into civic and investigative journalism, perhaps answering the question of what will happen when newspapers can no longer stay in business.

As the publishing industry is remade, change is the only constant. But that also creates abundant opportunities in book writing, as well as with print and online publications.

New technology is making self-publication a feasible, inexpensive, and even respectable option for many writers, particularly in nonfiction. Many experts believe self-publishing is the future of publishing altogether. Print-on-demand technology, which takes an electronic file like an Adobe PDF and instantly turns it into a book, makes publishing your novel or memoir both inexpensive and accessible.

A company called On Demand Books has developed a machine—the Espresso Book Machine—that converts digital files into bound books in about fifteen minutes. The whole process costs about a penny a page. Only a handful of Espresso machines were in use around the country in 2009, mostly at college bookstores, where students can order, say, an old textbook or century-old classic. Then, On Demand Books signed an agreement with Google to provide access to more than two million public domain titles, more than doubling the number of titles available through Espresso. And the American Booksellers Association (ABA) offered a POD program for booksellers who don't want to invest in an Espresso Machine. The ABA's Print-to-Order program allows stores to sell out-of-print or self-published books through a copublishing arrangement with Applewood Books of Carlisle, Massachusetts, which primarily produces backlist titles.

Amazon.com has gained strength with its own publishing and distribution companies, not to mention its electronic book reader, Kindle. E-book device sales took off, with several competing versions flooding the market. SONY has the Reader, Barnes & Noble brought out the Nook in late 2009, and Apple shook up the entire industry when it introduced its new iPad in February 2010.

While sales of print publications stagnate, their online presences are attracting record numbers of readers. A Nielsen Online analysis done for the Newspaper Association of America found in 2009 that newspaper Web sites had more than seventy million unique readers, representing nearly 36 percent of all Internet users. For many writers, Internet-based publications and social networking options offer new ways to both make money and connect with a reading public.

> Print-on-demand technology, which takes an electronic file like an Adobe PDF and instantly turns it into a book, makes publishing your novel or memoir both inexpensive and accessible.

And while the big publishing houses order cutbacks, the smaller presses, the academic, regional, and specialty (niche) houses, are—

if not growing—at least thriving. For a midlist writer, these smaller, independent publishers can offer attention and support that would be unlikely at the larger houses. There's a tradeoff: Advances are often minuscule, if they exist at all. But royalty percentages are often higher, which is of greater benefit to authors whose books sell well. Smaller presses also have a nimbleness uncommon among the big companies, which allows them to move quickly to cut expenses, if need be, or to take advantage of new technology.

By late 2009, the big publishers were beginning to embrace new technologies and the opportunities they afford. Macmillan expanded its audiobook offerings by selling podcasts. Penquin Group's CEO John Makinson announced his company views the new iPad platform as an opportunity to create a whole new kind of book, with streaming video, audio, and gaming incorporated into everything they publish. Thomas Nelson Books now bundles multiple formats of books and offers them for one price. Nelson President and CEO Michael S. Hyatt told *Publishers Weekly*, "I believe that the industry is shifting and we, as publishers, need to explore new methods of getting our content into the hands of customers."

Multimedia platforms have been embraced by children's book publishers, which find a ready and willing audience of young readers far more tech-savvy than their parents. Titles might be linked to a Web site or online contest, video game, playing cards, or other features intended to draw the kids into an entire media universe based on the book.

Amid all these changes is another uncertainty: how the massive Authors Guild settlement with Google, still being played out in the courts as this book goes to press, will turn out. Everyone in the publishing industry will be affected, not least the authors whose rights are at issue. The Authors Guild, joined by the Association of American Publishers, filed a class action lawsuit against Google after Google announced in 2004 that it planned to scan book content and create an electronic database of those works without the permission of, or payment to, authors or publishers.

Called the Google Library Project, Google had reached agreement with several libraries to scan and display portions of their books, many of them copyrighted. Google claimed that displaying small portions of the works online was allowed under the fair use doctrine of copyright law. The Authors Guild and AAP disagreed.

The proposed settlement would require Google to make a one-time payment of $34.5 million to establish and maintain a book rights registry to locate authors and manage payments to them from Google. Google would then pay rights holders 63 percent of all revenues from the database, and pay another $45 million to authors and publishers for works it had scanned into the database without permission prior to May 5, 2009. The settlement would also give authors and publishers the right to determine whether and to what extent Google can use their work. By late 2009, the proposed settlement had come under attack from a number of sources, including groups of individual authors, libraries, and even Amazon.com.

As writers, there is nothing more valuable to you than your intellectual rights. Any writing you create is protected by copyright law, whether you go through the process of registering the work or not. Technology can be a huge benefit to writers, but as the Google lawsuit shows, it also can be used to take advantage.

In the end, your career as a writer is in your hands. This book is intended to help you sort through the changes that have wracked the publishing industry and which continue to mold and change how it does business. Learn everything you can about the craft, consider all criticism, and read everything, especially the books that contain the kind of writing you aspire to. Inform yourself about the industry. Believe in yourself and your gifts, be persistent, and keep writing.

1. The Future of Publishing

"A writer is a person for whom writing is more difficult than it is for other people."—Thomas Mann

After talking with more than two dozen publishing world experts about what to expect in coming years, several trends emerged: Technology will continue to change and shape the industry; the big publishing houses will continue to cut back on the number of titles produced in the traditional fashion; smaller publishers will thrive as the big houses diminish; and it will be harder for unknown authors to get their work published, so more writers will turn to self-publishing to achieve their goals.

TECHNOLOGY-DRIVEN CHANGE

Emerging technology is driving some of the most sweeping shifts in how books and other media are published, how writers interact with the publishing industry, and how readers and other consumers get information.

Print-on-demand (POD) technology has made self-publishing both easy and more acceptable, forcing traditional publishers to rethink how they do business. Collaborations between traditional publishers and online publishing services are pushing the envelope, and in some cases prompting outcry. When Harlequin announced in late 2009 that it was teaming with the online publishing company

Author Solutions to allow romance writers to self-publish under a new imprint called Harlequin Horizons, the Romance Writers of America (RWA) cried foul. RWA immediately announced that Harlequin books would no longer be eligible for RWA contests. The Mystery Writers of America and Science Fiction and Fantasy Writers of America followed suit. Within days, Harlequin changed the name of its self-publishing arm to DellArte Press and removed all references to Harlequin from the new imprint's Web site.

Online magazines, blogs, social network sites like Facebook, MySpace, Linked-In, and Twitter, directly influence—and in some cases have drastically altered—how we communicate, how books and other media are published and distributed, and how new media are marketed.

Many writers are finding their first big breaks through online literary sites like Fictionaut (fictionaut.com) and McSweeney's Internet Tendency (mcsweeneys.net).

Fictionaut bills itself as "a literary community for adventurous readers and writers." Members can post their own fiction, poetry, or other writing on the site and receive feedback from other writers.

"I read Fictionaut every week, which publishes short stories by, I presume, young writers," says Victoria Skurnick, an agent with Levine Greenberg Literary Agency in New York. "I regularly go after the authors who seem talented. And there are clever (and entrepreneurial) writers who manage to get their work out there to masses of people without the benefit of a publisher."

McSweeney's Internet Tendency, an offshoot of award-winning writer Dave Eggers' publishing company, McSweeney's, also features fiction from aspiring writers. Sarah Schmelling's *Ophelia Joined the Group Maidens Who Don't Float*, which was based on a piece Schmelling wrote for McSweeney's, was published by Penguin imprint Plume. It had received more than 250,000 hits on the online site, *Publisher's Weekly* reported.

Similarly, in fall 2008, Thomas Dunne Books bought David Wong's urban fantasy, *John Dies at the End*, which had been read by more than 70,000 people at his online site, johndiesattheend.com.

Writers who employ new technologies to get their work into print are ahead of the curve. At some point, probably not too far into the future, almost everything published will move to an online format.

Michael Todd, editor of the online version of *Miller-McCune* magazine, explains:

> In the long run Kindle—or whatever the iPod-equivalent of the technology Kindle now represents becomes—is the future for all levels of publishing. Allow me to present a scenario: I'm walking down the street with an electronic device that fits in my pocket, but which contains either a screen or a way or projecting words that I can read in most light situations or when lying on my back. The price of the device was cheap enough that if I lose it, I'm not devastated, but it's expensive enough that I'm careful with it. (Think iPod.)
>
> Online magazines, blogs, social network sites like Facebook, MySpace, Linked-In and Twitter, directly influence—and in some cases have drastically altered—how we communicate.
>
> As I walk, I pass a handful of newspaper stands. There aren't actual papers in them, but electronic bulletin boards. I like a couple of headlines that flash by on one of them, and so I press a button on my device while waving over a certain piece of the newsstand. It uploads the day's content into my device's memory while subtracting a very minimal amount from either my bank account or a media escrow account I fund periodically (no pun intended). If I enter an area without WiFi, I can still read my "paper." If I'm in an area with WiFi, my stories are updated until my day's license expires.
>
> If I go to a bookstore, it's the same procedure. There will probably be a few proper books for me to examine, but it's

button-pushing time when I want something. The price point needs to be set where it's just as easy to buy as pirate the text, and perhaps there are some gew-gaws attached that make buying a more attractive option.

Unlike my newspaper, the book will probably remain on the hard drive until I manually delete it, although it may be that the book will reside elsewhere most of the time and my purchase merely allows me to access the work on a server elsewhere.

BIG HOUSES IN DECLINE

This shift to technology-driven publishing is closely tied to losses among traditional publishers, particularly the big publishing companies.

"There is no doubt the industry is consolidating and fewer books are being published by traditional publishers," Random House editor-at-large David Ebershoff says. "This is causing a great deal of disruption for many people—not just writers, but also agents, publishers, editors, designers, sales and marketing people, and booksellers. This is happening for many reasons, but the overarching reason is hardly a mystery—fewer people are reading books. More and more people are spending their free time and money on other activities—movies, TV, games, and especially Web surfing."

R.R. Bowker, an independent firm that tracks publishing data, reported in May 2009 that the number of fiction titles produced by traditional publishers dropped by 11 percent in 2008, with 47,541 new titles published. Total book output decreased by 3.2 percent in 2008, with 275,232 new titles and editions published, down from 284,370 in 2007. The number of books published by nontraditional means (self-publishing, both print-on-demand (POD) and short-run) increased a staggering 132 percent, with 285,394 POD titles published.

Kelly Gallagher, vice president of publisher services for Bowker, said in a company press release: "The statistics from 2008 are not just an indicator that the industry had a decline in new titles coming to the market, but they're also a reflection of how publishers are getting smarter and more strategic about the specific kinds of books they're choosing to publish. If you look beyond the numbers, you begin to see that 2008 was a pivotal year that benchmarks the changing face of publishing."

Josh Conviser, a screenwriter and author of the fantasy thrillers *Echelon* and *Empyre*, believes we're approaching a fundamental shift in how the publishing industry perceives itself:

> In order to survive and grow, publishers are going to have to accept and embrace the fact that books aren't the dominant creative platform. What does this mean? I think publishers will come to see that they are not in the business of selling books. They are in the business of creating intellectual property.
>
> Yes, selling books is of fundamental importance, but that's just one slice of the pie. Film, television, graphic novel, and video game rights make up the rest of the cake, not to mention foreign markets. The term "ancillary rights" is misleading. These markets are no longer of lesser importance. They should have equal weight to the right to publish the book itself. It's my belief that publishers will get more involved in all possible outlets for the books under their banner.

Conviser says this is already happening in the comic book/graphic novel world, where publishers in that market see their output as the starting point for building a multi-platform franchise: "A great comic can lead to a movie, to a video game, and on down the line. The publishers actively work these angles, and then take their cut of each media outlet their product breaks into."

> "There is no doubt the industry is consolidating and fewer books are being published by traditional publishers."—editor David Ebershoff

What does this mean for writers?

Doris Booth, manager of Authorlink Literary Group in Dallas, Texas, says, "There will be greater emphasis upon 'packaging' content. That is, the printed book will often be seen as part of a total package that can be easily adapted into other formats, including e-books, iPod downloads, movies, television programs, and even miniseries on the Internet. Content will need to be such that it can be broken into shorter bits for the purposes of promotion and/or serialization. Not that this will necessarily mean novels will be shorter, just suitable-for-digesting chunks. The style of writing must be more readily accessible—shorter chapters, quicker pace, without losing the sense of the story or the beauty of prose."

Conviser believes the transition will be both good and bad:

"The nature of our agreements with publishers will shift. We will give up more rights when we sign our contracts. A new formula will have to be created to take this into account. Book contracts will come to look more like those screenwriters sign on selling a script. For bestselling novelists, this will be an unwelcome shift and, as they have serious power, one that will be slow in coming."

But Conviser says the rest of us will benefit:

"Instead of trying to sell our ancillary rights as very small fish in a turbulent ocean, we will have a major company taking on the task. This means that we minnows will have a better chance of seeing our books picked up by Hollywood and the rest, which, in turn, means we'll sell more books. Giving up some control and profit participation in the bargain is well worth such benefits."

Conviser believes this new paradigm will also shift the major publishers' buying habits. Editors will seek not only quality manuscripts, but those that have the chance of becoming the basis for a franchise. "All this will lead to a greater symbiosis between publishing and other creative industries," he says.

Hollywood is already clamoring for product, says Conviser, who was executive consultant on the HBO series *Rome*: "In these uncertain times, most production companies feel more secure buying a project with underlying rights. Picking up the rights to a book means that they own something concrete and finished in its own right."

New formats will also challenge the traditional publishing model.

"Apple's new iPad will do for books what the iPod did for music," Conviser says. "It will put a tremendous strain on traditional booksellers. I don't think it will decimate them in the way music sellers got hit because there will always be readers who want the hard copy. There are just going to be fewer of us."

"The current method of spraying the market with way too many books and then sitting back and seeing what sticks doesn't work for anyone, including the writer."

Jeff Herman, of Jeff Herman Literary Agency, says: "What we see is a consolidation of patterns that began more than fifteen years ago, which is basically the round-up of independently owned publishers into global communication conglomerates, in which the book publishing programs are a very small part of the total revenue pie. The effect is that publishing decisions are deeply influenced by the shareholder's financial interests, as opposed to a measured balance between artistic and commercial factors."

Major publishers will become more selective in what they acquire, Doris Booth adds. They will also publish far fewer titles in printed format, partly because of the high cost of producing and selling a printed title, and also because of cutbacks in consumer spending.

> "The current method of spraying the market with way too many books and then sitting back and seeing what sticks doesn't work for anyone, including the writer."
>
> —author Josh Conviser

"Every year there are more books published but about the same or fewer sold," remarks Bay Tree Publishing Company owner David

Cole. "Beyond the few big winners, most writers, even professionals, earn an insignificant amount of money from their writing. Books provide the worst returns. This, however, does not seem to discourage people. Clearly the rewards of being a published author transcend monetary considerations, and, perhaps, this is as it should be. This will eventually change as a greater percentage of the population grows up caring more about other forms of communication than books, but that is a matter of decades, not a few years."

Smaller Presses Will Thrive

Independent book publishers will reap rewards, as the large houses cut back, says Paul Fedorko, an agent who heads the literary arm of New York City-based N.S. Bienstock, Inc:

"If a major publisher had ten imprints and now they have seven, it's a greater opportunity for an indie publisher. Some of those books that would have gone to a big house might be available to the smaller independent press. Ultimately you just want to get the book published. I just made a deal with a small publisher I had never heard of before."

Independent presses known for their quality (such as Graywolf Press) will become a more attractive secondary market for titles the larger publishers overlooked, and they may be able to increase their market share of sales in the years ahead, Booth says.

Victoria Skurnick also foresees small publishing houses like regional and special-interest presses emerging, which will widen the market.

Laurie Abkemeier, a nonfiction agent with DeFiore and Company of New Jersey, agrees: "A lot of publishers got imprint-happy over the last five years, so seeing some of them go by the wayside isn't necessarily a bad thing."

There are some terrific independent publishers who bring a lot of creativity to the table when it comes to packaging and promotion, Abkemeier says. Algonquin, Ten Speed, Chronicle, Running Press, and Sasquatch have all made reputations for themselves by translating vision into success. This book is published by an independent press with Book-of-the-Month Club selections, a *New York Times* bestseller, and a reputation for solid books on writing and becoming a published author.

"It would be great if publishers would all make room in their lists for authors with great potential, but that's become the domain of smaller houses," Abkemeier says. "There is simply too much competition for the slots at the major publishers that want to take on a lot of risk."

For the right projects, academic presses, like the University of California Press or the University of Michigan Press, also will become a more viable publishing option.

Karin Finell's memoir of growing up under the Third Reich and the devastating effects of World War II, *Goodbye to the Mermaids: A Childhood Lost in Hitler's Berlin*, was published by the University of Missouri Press in 2006. Finell, a longtime Santa Barbara Writers Conference alumna, chose the university press quite by accident:

"I met a woman at a luncheon whose friend was the chief editor of the University of Missouri Press, and who, so she told me, was interested in World War II and Hitler. When, after a few tries with other publishing houses, my agent had not placed the book, I sent it to this editor. My agent then placed it with her officially. He was able to retain film rights and other rights. Sadly, we did not specify electronic rights at that time, which are necessary today. And so far the press has resisted putting it on Kindle, which is too bad."

> For the right projects, academic presses, like the University of California Press or the University of Michigan Press, will become a viable publishing option.

Even so, Finell was thrilled with the university press:

"They treated me royally, gave me as much publicity as their budget could muster, never lied about anything, and were just wonderful to work with. They published an 'A' book. When they created a cover with colors I had suggested, buyers at Book Expo America told them the cover would not sell this book, and so they went back to the drawing board. A young woman at UMP designed the new cover, which came out terrific."

Finell says while you get paid, you won't get rich publishing with a university press:

> You also have to jump through many hoops; my book had to get final approval by two professors in the field, outside of the university. Then it had to be approved by a committee of professors within the university.
>
> The prestige of getting your first book published and later placed in university libraries and taught in several courses at universities makes up for the lack of compensation. But, of course, not every book lends itself to university publishing. In my case, it was lucky the book dealt with World War II and Hitler.

Unfortunately, universities feel the pinch of economics as well as everyone else, and many academic presses at the time of this writing were cutting back. But if you are looking for a more personal experience with a reputable publisher, university presses offer a good option, especially for historical nonfiction, biography, and memoir.

MORE WRITERS WILL SELF-PUBLISH

Probably the most significant trend for writers in coming years will be the option to self-publish.

Dan Poynter, who is often called the "Guru of Self-publishing," believes the current revolution in publishing will permanently alter the playing field, empowering writers and allowing them to put their work directly into the hands of the reading public. Who needs an agent and a publisher? If an author can write a good book, why shouldn't he or she reap 100 percent of the financial rewards?

Poynter's book, *The Self-Publishing Manual* (parapublishing.com), first appeared in 1979 and has gone through more than fifteen editions. The latest update includes information on new technologies and ways to use social networking and other Internet-based services to market your book.

"Authors will be closer to readers, especially in nonfiction," Poynter says. "E-books will reduce production costs and speed distribution. The reader will benefit because nonfiction will be fresher (not out of date yet). POD (print-on-demand) will eliminate large inventories. There are six large publishers in New York, 300–400 medium-sized publishers and 86,000 self-publishers in the United States. Only the small publishers will survive."

With this elimination of most of the gatekeepers, Poynter believes wholesalers and distributors are likely to disappear, as well. There will be no need for agents in the future. And editing will be very important: "People will not read crap. Writing has to be good," Poynter says.

"People buy nonfiction to learn something or to solve a problem," Poynter continues. "Four hundred thousand titles are published each year. Nonfiction is becoming more targeted, more specific. Writers will get to research and write about specific areas—those that interest them.

> "Authors will be closer to readers, especially in nonfiction. E-books will reduce production costs and speed distribution. The reader will benefit because nonfiction will be fresher (not out of date yet). POD (print-on-demand) will eliminate large inventories."
>
> —publisher and author Dan Poynter

"The handwriting is on the wall. Traditional publishing is shackled with returns, the three-season selling system, publication dates, large advances, and increased transportation costs."

In the end, there will be fewer books without a market, he adds. Writers will concentrate on material that people want to buy as opposed to what agents and acquisition editors think readers will buy. And feedback will come electronically at the speed of light.

"Clearly, the Internet combined with print-on-demand has transformed the self-publishing industry," says Ivory Madison, founder of the author-marketing site RedRoom.com. "It allows hobbyist authors and 'indie authors' to produce their own books easily, affordably, and with a level of quality that wasn't possible just a few years ago.

"It's really amazing and exciting how professional the result can be for self-published authors now. In the next three years, the leading self-publishing companies will virtually perfect the software, process, and pricing models to the point where you can achieve exactly your vision for any book you want—for free."

She thinks of self-published authors in four categories, the first three of which are: hobbyists who want to create a book for self-expression, gifts, or personal interest; indie authors who are legitimate writers who cannot find an editor at a publishing house who believes their book could be commercially successful; and those who think they are in the previous category but their work really is awful and shouldn't be published.

The fourth category has been statistically insignificant but will grow in coming years: authors who have an offer from a legitimate publishing house but elect to self-publish anyway, as a creative and business decision.

"This last category is the only one that could conceivably affect the publishing industry in any way. I believe the publishers will adapt rather than lose this business," Madison says.

The thing to remember, as a writer, is the changing landscape offers opportunities as well as challenges.

2. An Uncertain World for Fiction Writers

"Writing a novel is like driving a car at night. You can only see as far as your headlights, but you can make the whole trip that way."
—*E. L. Doctorow*

For all the uncertainty in publishing today, perhaps no writers feel it as intensely as those who write fiction. Novel and short story writing is a tough business to break into in the first place. Add to that a writer's natural insecurities and the flux in the current market, and you have a situation that appears dire. There's no question that selling fiction is more difficult today than previously. Not impossible, but difficult.

As the big publishing houses have reduced the number of new fiction titles they acquire, self-published fiction has increased. The Internet has opened up opportunities for new novelists to connect with a reading public and to sell their work directly to readers. Blogging, personal Web sites, and social networking now allow writers to promote and sell their novels without a publisher's traditional marketing efforts.

"This doesn't mean the book is dead or even dying," editor David Ebershoff says:

> It just means that more than ever before, a book needs to assert its relevance. At the same time, publishers need to focus on amplifying that relevance. Everyone in this industry—from

the writer at the keyboard to the editor at the desk beneath
the lamp to the bookseller on the frontline—will need to work
harder to make books relevant to our day.

This can, and does, happen. Look at Cormac McCarthy's
The Road. This book matters to our culture in a highly unique
way. The experience of reading it, and the lessons drawn
from it, cannot be found elsewhere. It has no trouble competing with YouTube or CNN or Facebook. Stephenie Meyers is
another writer who has found a way to write books that assert
themselves vigorously in our crazy, overloaded, no-free-time,
book-disinclined culture. In nonfiction, David McCullough
does this. Same with Malcolm Gladwell. They are just four
examples. There are many, many more. These successes have
many factors, including luck and robust publishing campaigns.
But there is a common denominator: Each writes books people
want to read.

The truth is that good books will always be published, agent
Victoria Skurnick says. "There is no reason to quit just because everyone, myself included, is talking about how hard it is. If you have
something original to say, to explore, to investigate, chances are you
can still make your way to getting yourself heard. And, in this electronic age, you can be heard without the help of a big publisher. It is
less financially rewarding, of course, but now you can accomplish a
lot with your own talent and energy. No one has to go unheard."

Every agent I talked with—in fact, every person I interviewed
for this book—emphasized that a story told well will always find its
way to publication.

"Editors routinely troll Web sites and publications on the subjects
they have interest in," Ebershoff says. "News magazines [look] for a
particular kind of writing, the political blogs for another, the sports
Web sites and blogs for sports-related books. Sometimes I'll just be
reading and it will prompt an idea and I might contact the writer to
say, 'Have you ever thought of writing a book?' "

For fiction, the task is to write the best manuscript you can and
get it to the right agent, Ebershoff says.

Best-selling author Catherine Ryan Hyde launched what became a very successful adult and young adult fiction writing career by submitting short stories to literary magazines. Ryan Hyde, who, early on in her writing endeavors attended the Santa Barbara Writers Conference, is best-known for her novel *Pay it Forward*, which was made into a major motion picture. She has since written twelve novels, seven for young adults.

> Every agent I talked with—in fact, every person I interviewed for this book—emphasized that a story told well will always find its way to publication.

"I can't stress too strongly the importance of hammering out a few publishing credits on your own," Ryan Hyde says. "When I first started writing novels, I couldn't get an agent to look at anything I'd done. I queried between twenty-five and thirty agents with my first novel, and not one single agent wanted to see anything more from me. Not even sample chapters.

"So I started writing short stories and marketing them myself."

After Hyde had three short stories published, and one was honored in the Raymond Carver contest, she decided to query five more agents with both her first and second novels. All five asked for both manuscripts.

However, "I got my first agent at the Santa Barbara Writers Conference," Ryan Hyde says. "We had some mutual friends. I handed her two small-circulation literary magazines with my stories in them, and then a few days later asked her if I could send thirty pages of my novel. Her answer? No, just send me the whole manuscript, because I already know that I like the way you write."

That agent didn't sell her novels, though.

"I had a story published in the tiny and now defunct literary magazine *Bottomfish*. A month or two later, an agent wrote me a letter of solicitation."

The magazine had come into the agent's hands because one of her other clients, who had published a story in the same issue, had given her a copy. She read Ryan Hyde's story and was impressed enough to ask if she was seeking representation.

Ryan Hyde signed with her, and that agency sold her first five novels and made her first three movie deals.

"Don't expect that you will quickly get an agent who will do all the tough marketing work for you," Ryan Hyde says. "Be prepared to prove yourself through smaller publishing credits. The more you can distinguish yourself, by proving both that you are writing at a publishable level and that you are willing to work hard on the business end of your career, the better."

Thinking creatively, and being willing to take a risk, helped both Ron McLarty and N. Frank Daniels realize their publication dreams.

Ron McLarty's first novel, *The Memory of Running* (2005), was originally published as an audiobook, and it took off after Stephen King described it as "The best book you can't read."

"I wrote ten novels (and forty-four plays) over a thirty-year span," McLarty says. "Although I felt they were quite good, I fell between the agent/publishing cracks. About ten or so years ago, I was recording an audiobook for Recorded Books—a company that sells to libraries and online. A lightbulb snapped on and I asked if I might record one of my own novels for their catalog. They agreed, but only after I promised to narrate several more for them for free! So they put *The Memory of Running*, with me narrating, directly onto CD and into their catalogue. Naturally no one rented it, as I was unknown as an author."

More than ten years later, McLarty was auditioning for a TV show in New York. "I gave a pretty poor reading and wanted to get out quickly when this hand grabbed my arm. It belonged to Stephen King—he asked me if I was Ron McLarty, the novelist! It seems that King, during his convalescence from an auto accident, was browsing the Recorded Books catalogue and saw my name.

"I rushed to Recorded Books and begged them to send him a copy. Then, quite honestly, I forgot all about it—my natural reaction to those many years of sending things out and never getting a response."

Several months later, McLarty was driving from New York to Los Angeles to do a couple of TV shows. "I got a call that Stephen King had not only listened to my book on CD but he had devoted his entire column, 'The Pop of King' in *Entertainment Weekly*, to my book. He titled it, 'The Best Book You Can't Read,' and proceeded to praise my novel and also take the publishing world to task for a missed opportunity.

"By the time I reached L.A., I had an agent and everyone wanted to read the book." Seven publishing houses bid on the book at auction. McLarty relates:

> Penguin/Viking bought it for more than I could have imagined even in my wildest dreams. Then it sold to fourteen countries at the Frankfurt Bookfair (and we got invited to visit Ireland, the United Kingdom, Holland, Norway, Sweden, Australia, and New Zealand when they published the book). It also sold to Warner Brothers.
>
> Miracles are funny things. Some of my friends said they were sorry I had to wait so long, but I think the timing was perfect. I was 55 when I entered the publishing fray, thrilled and excited and humble. If I had had this event happen when I was 35, I probably would have made the mistake of thinking I deserved it!

> "By the time I reached L.A., I had an agent and everyone wanted to read the book."—author Ron McLarty

He does deserve it. McLarty came to the Santa Barbara Writers Conference in 2006 and wowed audiences with his story about getting published. In fact, it was the first time in a long while that a speaker won a standing ovation at SBWC. He followed *The Memory of Running* with *Traveler*, published by Viking in 2007. His third novel, *Art in America*, came out in 2008.

Frustrated with the barriers to traditional book publication, N. Frank Daniels got his novel, *futureproof*, published after posting fifty pages of it on his MySpace page in February 2006. He promoted it like crazy online, and then he self-published using print-on-demand technology. Soon *futureproof* was gaining not only attention, but accolades. The novel was a top-five finalist for PODdy Mouth's 2006 Needle Award, was featured in *Entertainment Weekly* and the New York press, and it received an "A" rating by the print-on-demand reviewer PODler. It garnered raves from readers and established writers alike. Soon it caught the attention of editors at HarperPerennial, which published it in January 2009.

"While *futureproof* is being trumpeted as a self-published success that found a big enough audience to warrant a chance for a larger audience, the truth is that my experience of living this authors' dream is far from isolated," Daniels wrote in his blog. "I'm not the first writer to have found his way into mainstream publishing by using the self-publishing route. I will not be the last; not by a long shot. As the entire publishing industry is shaken to its core by the current economic climate, a completely new publishing paradigm is taking root.

"Yes, I carried copies of my self-published book around in the trunk of my car, but the great majority of my book sales came from people buying it off of Amazon and other electronically connected booksellers."

While it's important to acknowledge new ways to expose your work, it's equally important not to give up on traditional publishing possibilities.

"If you are agented, it makes sense to pitch the big houses. They are still looking for the next big thing," says Doris Booth, manager of Authorlink Literary Group in Dallas, Texas. "Yes, there is an overemphasis upon celebrity books. But editors still seek the next Harry Potter, or Stephanie Plumb, or Dan Brown."

Brown wrote a nonfiction book with his now-wife in 1995 titled *187 Men to Avoid: A Guide for the Romantically Frustrated Woman*, which drew little or no attention. Then, in 1996, *The Da Vinci Code* sold 6,000 copies on the first day of its release.

"So, I think the right idea and the right author who writes extremely well still has a shot at the big publishing house," Booth says. "It's just a tougher game. And you have to be plenty tough to persevere through a lot of rejection. The point is we never know what the next big book will be."

Ken Atchity, founder of Atchity Entertainment International of Los Angeles, says:

> Prioritize what you write and attempt to publish. High concept, brand-able, market-friendly (which means the market needs it) projects should be done now, not your more esoteric, ego-centered projects. Save those till you're well-known, and then publish them if you're still interested. Get business-serious about your writing, especially if you want it to support you.
>
> I recommend finding a public domain classic that has not been adopted into a novel, or a screenplay, and doing a bang-up job of it. That way you're not just asking them to read the Unknown You, you're asking them to read Shakespeare or Marlowe. That will get you in the door! Or, come up with a concept for your book or script that is franchisable, as Ian Fleming did with his 007. The challenge is that it must seem fresh and original. If you do either, please think of me first!

Remember that success builds on itself.

"If you've already been published and you have a good track record, the publisher will continue with you," agent Paul Fedorko says. "But if your sales start to decline, it gets harder and harder to get them to buy your books. A first novel, whatever it might be, has a better chance because there's no track record. It's based on it being good or bad. If that curve starts going down, though, it's really tough. Economics are bad, and publishers just don't have room on their lists for an author whose books don't return on investment."

If the publisher paid you a healthy advance expecting your book to sell 100,000 copies and it sold 20,000 copies, that publisher is not apt to give you a contract for Book Two, Booth agrees. "Your track record can bite you. The trick is to make sure the size of your advance reflects realistic expectations for the sale. A huge advance is not always the best way to build a career."

Still, this is an era of change.

"Who knows what will really happen, what good trends may emerge with the bad?" agent Victoria Skurnick says. "There is always the possibility that one man's midlist is another man's potential bestseller. You can't give up before even approaching the gate."

3. First, Write a Good Book (Honing Your Work)

"Writing is easy: All you do is sit staring at a blank sheet of paper until drops of blood form on your forehead."—Gene Fowler

What is good writing? It is both art and craft. Talent means nothing if the writer has not mastered the craft of writing—that is, knowing the specifics of sentence structure, grammar, punctuation, and the more subtle factors that make writing readable, even enjoyable, such as clarity, simplicity, and tone of voice. Good writing flows and has a lyrical quality. It includes detail that touches our senses, has drama, and uses language that is a pleasure to absorb.

There are five characteristics of good writing:

- precision
- clarity
- concreteness
- sensory appeal
- uses of figures of speech

Precision means using the right word for the job. Know the precise meanings of words, and choose the ones that express exactly what it is you want to convey.

Simplicity, correct grammar and punctuation, and coherence (meaning the writing has a logical structure, sentence by sentence, paragraph by paragraph) will make your writing clear and understandable. Most of your sentences should be based on a simple subject-verb-object formula. Sentences that are relatively short make your writing understandable. But don't fall into the trap of using only short sentences; varying sentence length adds interest and makes the writing flow. Avoid jargon and clichés. If you experiment with story structure, incorporate flashbacks, or begin *in medias res* (Latin for "in the midst of affairs"), it has to make sense. If it doesn't, the reader will leave.

Be concrete: Use descriptive detail and be specific. Include solid facts, not generalizations, and avoid abstract writing.

Incorporate the senses. Consider the following excerpt from Sandra Cisneros' *The House on Mango Street*:

> Most likely I will go to hell and most likely I deserve to be there. My mother says I was born on an evil day and prays for me. Lucy and Rachel pray too. For ourselves and for each other…because of what we did to Aunt Lupe.
>
> Her name was Guadalupe and she was pretty like my mother. Dark. Good to look at. In her Joan Crawford dress and swimmer's legs. Aunt Lupe of the photographs.
>
> But I knew her sick from the disease that would not go, her legs bunched under the yellow sheets, the bones gone limp as worms. The yellow pillow, the yellow smell, the bottles and spoons. Her head thrown back like a thirsty lady. My aunt, the swimmer.
>
> Hard to imagine her legs once strong, the bones hard and parting water, clean sharp strokes, not bent and wrinkled like a baby, not drowning under the sticky yellow light. Second-floor rear apartment. The naked light bulb. The high ceilings. The light bulb always burning.

Can you see Aunt Lupe? Can you smell her? Are you in that room, amid all the yellow? Do you see the bare light bulb hanging from the ceiling? Cisneros puts you there.

Good writing appeals to one or more of the five senses: touch, smell, taste, hearing, vision. If you write a scene about going out for pizza, include the smell as your characters walk in the front door of the pizzeria. Let your reader feel the heat from the wood-burning oven. Does it smell like a particular kind of wood, like mesquite? How would you describe the pizza parlor? What color are the walls? What kind of tables are there? Are they wooden picnic tables or Formica-topped rounds? Are they covered in red-and-white checkered clothes? Is music playing in the background? What kind? Is it loud or soft? What do the characters look like? How does the beer taste? Is it a pale lager or a dark, hearty ale? All of these details make for a richer, more interesting scene.

The following excerpt from Andrew Davidson's *The Gargoyle* is a good example of how one appeals to the senses in their writing:

> I remember the hot silver flash as the floorboard severed all my toes from my left foot. I remember the steering column sailing over my shoulder. I remember the eruption of glass that seemed to be everywhere around me. When the car finally came to a stop, I hung upside down, seatbelted. I could hear the hiss of various gases escaping the engine and the tires still spinning outside, above, and there was the creak of metal settling as the car stopped rocking, a pathetic turtle on its back.
>
> Just as I was beginning my drift into unconsciousness, there was the explosion. Not a movie explosion but a small real-life explosion, like the ignition of an unhappy gas oven that holds a grudge against its owner. A flash of blue flame skittered across the roof of the car, which was at a slanted angle underneath my dangling body. Out of my nose crawled a drop of blood, which jumped expectantly into the happy young flames springing to life beneath me. I could feel my hair catch fire; then I could smell it. My flesh began to singe as if I were a scrap of meat newly thrown onto the barbecue, and then I could hear the

Good writing appeals to one or more of the five senses: touch, smell, taste, hearing, vision.

bubbling of my skin as the flames kissed it. I could not reach my head to extinguish my flaming hair. My arms would not respond to my commands.

Davidson makes you believe you are the character, hanging upside down, skin incinerating as you watch, helpless. It's a horrific scene, and terrific writing.

And, finally, good writing incorporates figures of speech, which allow you to show contrasts and similarities. Using similes and metaphors helps readers develop a richer understanding of what's happened. A simile shows similarities by using the words "like" or "as" in describing something. It compares one thing to another: "Her smile sparkled like a bright star in a darkened universe." A metaphor uses one thing to represent or describe another: "Her smile was a bright star in a darkened universe."

There is grave danger in using trite or over-used metaphors and similes. They must be fresh to engage the reader. Davidson does this well in the above example: "a pathetic turtle rocking on its back" and "like the ignition of an unhappy gas oven that holds a grudge against its owner."

Consider this excerpt from *Their Eyes Were Watching God*, by Zora Neale Hurston:

> Janie awoke next morning by feeling Tea Cake almost kissing her breath away. Holding her and caressing her as if he feared she might escape his grasp and fly away. Then he must dress hurriedly and get to his job on time. He wouldn't let her get him any breakfast at all. He wanted her to get her rest. He made her stay where she was. In her heart she wanted to get his breakfast for him. But she stayed in bed long after he was gone.
>
> So much had been breathed out by the pores that Tea Cake still was there. She could feel him and almost see him bucking around the room in the upper air. After a long time of passive happiness, she got up and opened the window and let Tea Cake leap forth and mount to the sky on a wind. That was the beginning of things.

> In the cool of the afternoon the fiend from hell specially sent to lovers arrived at Janie's ear. Doubt. All the fears that circumstance could provide and the heart feel, attacked her on every side. This was a new sensation for her, but no less excruciating. If only Tea Cake would make her certain! He did not return that night nor the next and so she plunged into the abyss and descended to the ninth darkness where light has never been.

Vivid, concrete description. Sensory appeal. Figures of speech. All of these tools will improve your writing.

READ TO WRITE WELL

You should also build a good library of reference materials and books on writing. Some of my favorites include Anne LaMott's *Bird by Bird*, Stephen King's *On Writing: A Memoir of the Craft*, and Carolyn See's *Making a Literary Life*. See's book has the best advice on how to revise your work that I've read. And William Zinsser's *On Writing Well* is one of the best books on writing that exists.

Zinsser says: "Ultimately the product that any writer has to sell is not the subject being written about, but who he or she is. I often find myself reading with interest about a topic I never thought would interest me—some scientific quest, perhaps. What holds me is the enthusiasm of the writer for the field....This is the personal transaction that's at the heart of good nonfiction writing. Out of it come two of the most important qualities: humanity and warmth. Good writing has an aliveness that keeps the reader reading from one paragraph to the next, and it's not a question of gimmicks to 'personalize' the author. It's a question of using the English language in a way that will achieve the greatest clarity and strength."

While Zinsser was writing about nonfiction, I believe what he has to say also applies to good fiction.

Writing takes practice and lots of study. And, usually, many, many revisions. A first draft does not a novel make. Santa Barbara Writers Conference workshop leaders are accomplished authors who spend most of their workshop time providing feedback on work in progress. Many writers return to the conference year after year, honing, perfecting, rewriting. They listen, ask questions, read their work, and accept criticism. Ultimately, everything begins and ends with a well-written story.

What is story? One of my workshop leaders, Shelly Lowenkopf, can lecture on this topic for hours, day after day after day. I've seen him do it. Still, it's worth trying to quantify and express here briefly, because once you've mastered the basics of writing, a good story is what it's all about.

Does it have a compelling storyline? Are the characters believable and sympathetic? Is the dialogue realistic? Are the scenes vivid? Does the plot move the story along? Does the tension rise?

> "Ultimately the product that any writer has to sell is not the subject being written about, but who he or she is."
> —author William Zinsser

R. L. LaFevers, the author of six young adult novels, who teaches at the conference, once told me: "Put your protagonist into an impossible situation, and once he or she gets out of it, create another more perilous situation, and then do it again until you almost can't believe he or she will survive."

Consider Harry Potter. How many times does he barely escape before the final confrontation when he ultimately beats the villain ("He Who Must Not be Named")? That's called rising tension, and J. K. Rowling uses it masterfully throughout all seven books in the series.

"If you're a fiction writer, you are an entertainer first," says Bob Mayer, author of more than forty fiction and nonfiction books, many of them bestsellers. "But a trend is also to inform in fiction. So combining an intriguing subject matter with a fast-paced plot and distinctive characters is key."

Tim O'Brien, who wrote the luminous *The Things They Carried*, offered this advice in the *Atlantic Monthly*: "Above all, a well-imagined story is organized around extraordinary human behaviors and unexpected and startling events, which help illuminate the commonplace and the ordinary."

A "well-imagined" story. "Extraordinary human behaviors." "Unexpected and startling events." Think of Tolkien's trilogy, *The Fellowship of the Rings*, *The Two Towers*, and *The Return of the King*, my all-time favorite books. What happens to Frodo, the protagonist, in the three books? An ordinary Hobbit, with no discernible talents or courage, is called upon to perform the most extraordinary of tasks: to take a powerful and evil ring back to where it was forged and throw it into a cauldron of molten rock deep within a faraway mountain. To do so requires an arduous journey, full of perilous creatures and experiences, during which Frodo will be sorely tested, learn lessons about himself and others, and ultimately accomplish his task. It's a classic hero's journey. And, as O'Brien says, the commonplace and the ordinary are illuminated for us along the way.

"If you want to be a writer, you must do two things above all others: read a lot and write a lot," Stephen King says in *On Writing*. He adds:

> One learns most clearly what not to do by reading bad prose—one novel like *Asteroid Miners* (or *Valley of the Dolls*, *Flowers in the Attic*, and *The Bridges of Madison County*, to name just a few) is worth a semester at a good writing school, even with the superstar guest lecturers thrown in.

> Good writing, on the other hand, teaches the learning writer about style, graceful narration, plot development, the creation of believable characters, and truth-telling. A novel like *The Grapes of Wrath* may fill a writer with feelings of despair and good old-fashioned jealousy—'I'll never be able to write anything that good, not if I live to be a thousand'—but such feelings can also serve as a spur, goading the writer to work harder and aim higher.... So we read to experience the mediocre and the outright rotten; such experience helps us to recognize those things when they begin to creep into our own work, and to steer clear of them.

Francine Prose, whose book *Reading Like a Writer* is a delightful immersion into the world of reading and how that can make us all better writers, says:

> Though writers have learned from the masters in a formal methodical way…the truth is that this sort of education more often involves a kind of osmosis. After I've written an essay in which I've quoted at length from great writers, so that I've had to copy out long passages of their work, I've noticed that my own work becomes, however briefly, just a little more fluent.
>
> In the process of becoming a writer, I read and reread the authors I most loved. I read for pleasure, first, but also more analytically, conscious of style, of diction, of how sentences were formed and information was being conveyed, how the writer was structuring a plot, creating characters, employing detail and dialogue.
>
> What writers know is that, ultimately, we learn to write by practice, by hard work, by repeated trial and error, success and failure, and from the books we admire.

> "If you want to be a writer, you must do two things above all others: read a lot and write a lot."
>
> —author Stephen King

Many agents, when you ask them how you can best improve your work, will also say, "Read."

"Keep writing and practicing your craft and buy as many books as you can afford. The more you read the better you learn to write," says agent Bonnie Nadell. "There is no secret formula. No right answer that will get a writer a career. The best thing writers can do is try to shine in their writing and sooner or later someone will see their work and recognize their talent."

"You'd be surprised how many writers lose sight of how important it is that readers respond to the book," editor David Ebershoff says. "Storytelling is the core of what drives us to read. Another way of putting it is this: Write the best damn book you can. It all starts with the book. There is no better way for a writer to position himself or herself than writing a book people can't put down."

If you would spend $25 to buy your book, and give up twelve or fifteen hours with your family and friends to read it, then chances are someone else will want to read it, too, he says.

"Go to writers conferences, join writing groups…network, network, network," agent Paul Fedorko says. "With writers conferences, look for those with high-quality workshops and seminars. The people who are running those seminars, that's the key. When people walk out of that room and they say, 'I really got it,' those are the workshops you want to attend. Some instructors try to sell themselves so they can get a client out of it. To me, that's not the kind of instructor you want. You want someone whose primary goal is to help you become a better writer. That's an important factor, along with the quality of the teaching and the focus on giving writers some real info that informs and helps. The other thing that is always successful is to have real authors who teach."

Getting feedback on your work is crucial. "If you can find small-group settings, where the workshop is focused on reading each other's work and helping each other, that's part of the whole piece," Fedorko advises.

"In today's consolidated New York publishing industry, little time and money is spent on editing," agrees Ken Atchity, founder of Atchity Entertainment International in Los Angeles, a book packaging company. "If a manuscript comes in that requires editing to any degree, it is usually rejected in favor of the hundreds that a given publisher reads each year that are well-edited."

Many agents recommend you have a "book doctor" look over your manuscript before you send it off, and I agree this is a good idea, especially if you are weak in such line editing areas as grammar, spelling, and sentence structure. A good book doctor or editor can provide a studied perspective and often can point out story structure problems as well. It's worth the cost if it keeps an agent from tossing your manuscript aside because of a careless editing error or lapse in story structure, characterization, or dialogue.

Your writing must be absolutely sparkly and pristine. Revise, revise, revise. And seek help from experienced editors.

4. Agents, Advances, and Copyright

"A good many young writers make the mistake of enclosing a stamped, self-addressed envelope, big enough for the manuscript to come back in. This is too much of a temptation to the editor."
—*Ring Lardner*

In my experience, new writers are almost always the most eager and usually the most unprepared to give their work to an agent.

Barnaby Conrad, the founder of the Santa Barbara Writers Conference, loves to tell the story of the woman who came to SBWC one year. It was her first time at a writers conference and she was very excited about being there. But just a few days after the conference started, Barnaby saw her standing in front of the hotel, bags packed, waiting for a taxi. "Why are you leaving?" he asked. She replied: "It's been three days already and not one publisher has bought my book."

For an aspiring fiction writer, nothing seems more exciting—or more elusive—than the prospect of finding an agent and landing a book contract. While a nonfiction book's success depends on content, fiction is all about the writing and the story. That means a writer has to have a completed manuscript—polished to a high gleam—before any agent will even look at it, let alone try to sell it to a publisher.

"With fiction, you need an agent to get to an editor," David Ebershoff says. "The time it takes to review a manuscript, and the amount of screening that's necessary, makes it too time-consuming. Editors depend on agents to do that primary work. An agent is still the best way to have your work represented. With nonfiction, you can catch the eye of an editor by writing and getting something published, either on the Web or on a blog, or in news magazines. But an agent is always going to make the project better."

Almost to a person, brand-new writers who come to the writers conference with a first draft think they're ready to talk to agents. Like many other conferences, SBWC has an Agents and Editors Day devoted to one-on-one meetings between writers and agents. It's an opportunity for writers to pitch their projects to agents and editors, and every writer hopes to land that elusive representation contract. Some, I'm proud to say, have won representation and subsequently signed a book contract with a publisher. Most, however, learn a valuable lesson: Their books need a lot more work. Many also receive salient and specific advice from the agents as to how they can improve their work—or their pitch.

One year, a young woman attended the conference for the first time and on the first day signed up to pitch her novel to four different agents. Agents and Editors Day was four days away. By the third day, she was back at the sign-up table asking if someone else could take her spots with the agents. I asked why. She said, "I realized after being in the writing workshops that my book isn't close to being ready to be seen by an agent." I smiled. She had discovered what most writers who come to the conference discover. We can all improve our work.

Also, unlike with nonfiction, where you approach an agent or editor with a nonfiction book proposal, most agents won't consider a novel unless you've written the whole book. Someone with an exceptional writing talent may win representation on the strength of a few chapters. Bonnie Nadell offered to represent the late David Foster Wallace after he mailed a chapter of his first novel, *The Broom of the System*, to her. She was a brand-new agent at the time, and she sold his novel three months later to Penguin Books. Nadell was Wallace's agent for the remainder of his career. However, acquiring an agent with a single chapter is rare. If you have only the kernel of an idea and a chapter or two, you are wasting your time and the agent's time with a meeting or a query.

Many writers make the mistake of thinking that just because they've finished a manuscript it's ready for prime time. In all likelihood it's not. That's where "polishing to a high gleam" comes into play.

The manuscript has to be spotless in terms of grammar and spelling. If it is a novel, the story must be compelling and structured in such a way that it flows from the first

> Unlike with nonfiction where, you approach an agent or editor with a book proposal, most agents won't consider a novel unless you have a completed manuscript.

word, through rising levels of conflict, and right on to the final denouement. Primary characters must be vivid and three-dimensional. Dialogue must be realistic and interesting. If any of these things is missing, you're well-advised to go back to the drawing board and revise.

Nonfiction works must also be well written and accomplish what they set out to do. Go to writers conferences and get feedback on your work. Take writing courses. Join (or start) a writing group for ongoing critiques. Take the manuscript to a "book doctor," if necessary.

On the other hand, if you have done all the above, if you've gotten rave reviews from not just friends but from mentors, writing teachers, and authors whose work you admire, then you're ready to look for an agent.

But how do you get one? I wish I had a dollar for every time this question has been asked at SBWC. The Agents and Editors Panel at the conference is always the most popular event, and the agents and book editors who participate usually say something along the lines of: First, perfect your craft, *then* begin researching the market for an agent.

One way to locate an agent who specializes in your genre is to research other books that are similar to yours, then look at the acknowledgments in the books you like and note who the author thanks. Usually his or her agent will be among the first listed. Look the agent up on the Internet or in a current literary agent listing. My favorite is *Jeff Herman's Guide to Book Publishers, Editors and Literary Agents.* Jeff has spoken at the Santa Barbara Writers Conference and he contributed to this book, but I discovered his literary guide many years ago and have found it to be very helpful in determining what an agent's interests are and whether he or she might be a good fit for my current project. In addition to telling you how to query (Query letter with synopsis? First fifty pages? Nonfiction book proposal with the first three chapters? By e-mail or snail-mail, etc.), Herman's guide tells you an agent's hobbies and interests, and what kinds of things one can do to improve the chances of having a manuscript accepted.

> One way to locate an agent who specializes in your genre is to research other books that are similar to yours, then look at the acknowledgments in the books you like and note who the author thanks.

One way to connect with an agent (or editor) is to do a one-on-one meeting at a writers conference. It can be a little scary the first time you have to pitch your manuscript, but it's always to your advantage to do so, even if you only use the meeting as an opportunity to practice. You'll need a short, concise spiel that explains your project vividly and takes thirty seconds or less. Can you do this? If not, find a friend who will work with you and listen to you until you have it down to a science. Your short pitch should do three things: explain what the project is (novel? nonfiction? mystery? romance?), what it's about (this is the tough part), and why it should be published (compare it to others on the market). I have been working on a children's book for some time. Here's my elevator pitch (so called because you want to be prepared to deliver your pitch should you find yourself in an elevator with an agent or editor): "The title of my book is *A Hop, Skip and a Jump: The Adventures of MaryJane, the Bunny Who Couldn't Hop*. It's the story of a disabled bunny who helps a young teen comes to terms with the loss of her mother and life in a wheelchair. Like *The Velveteen Rabbit*, MaryJane finds a way to profoundly affect her human friend, but also to learn something about herself along the way."

Read the backs of some of the best contemporary novels to see examples of what would be good elevator pitches. How would some famous novels be described in thirty seconds? *Gone with the Wind* might be: "A Southern dilettante has her life high-jacked by the Civil War, which brings unbelievable hardship. In the end, she discovers her own gifts of fortitude and courage, but discovers, too late, what love truly is." Or, how about a pitch for *Jaws*? "A giant man-eating great white terrorizes a beach community, setting up an epic battle between the shark and the man summoned to destroy it." Try this with other well-known books and then write an elevator pitch for your own. It gets easier with practice, which will also give you confidence when you do meet with an agent.

Here are some other tips for surviving an agent meeting: Breathe. Really! If you take some deep breaths just before you sit down, you'll feel more relaxed and appear more relaxed. Don't apologize for being nervous. Agents know you are. Be positive. Exchange a few pleasantries, but be ready to give your pitch quickly and with confidence. Also be prepared to answer any questions the agent may have, for example, why is your project unique and how might it be marketed? What other titles in your genre have sold well, and how could that benefit your book? What is your writing experience?

Be prepared to give the agent a written synopsis of the novel, if he or she asks for it. (For nonfiction, you should have a written book proposal ready to go, which includes a project description, chapter outline, and at least one sample chapter. More on this in Chapter 5.)

The agent will tell you on the spot if he or she is interested. If not, be gracious, thank him or her for the time, and move on to another agent. Don't dwell on the rejection. Agents have individual tastes, and they know exactly what kind of book they seek. If one agent says no, the chances are good another will say yes. Don't get discouraged.

If the agent is interested, he or she is likely to ask you to send either several chapters or the entire manuscript. If this happens, you should say how delighted you are and promise to follow up. When your ten minutes are up, get up to leave. When you are safely out of sight, do an enthusiastic, happy dance. You're entitled; this is a very good thing! When you get home from the conference, follow up immediately, and include a nice note reminding the agent that he or she met you at such-and-such conference and requested your manuscript. Say you are anxious to hear what they think once they've had a chance to read the whole thing. Then wait. It typically takes an agent several months to respond to a query, though many will give your manuscript first priority if they requested it at a conference. If you don't hear from the agent after eight weeks, a phone call to inquire if he or she has had a chance to read it is absolutely fine. An e-mail also works. Always be professional and polite. The last thing you want to be is a pest, or worse, a potential client from hell. This includes people who phone repeatedly, resist suggestions for improvement, are egotistical know-it-alls, and/or insist on advances or accommodations that outmatch the work they've produced. Don't be a client from hell.

If you are querying agents via mail or e-mail, your elevator pitch can be a jumping-off point for writing a good query letter. The main points to remember are to make it brief, compelling, informative, and persuasive. It should begin with what is widely known as the "hook"—a first paragraph that describes the book or concept in a way that really grabs the attention of the agent. This is where your elevator pitch comes in handy.

After the hook, the letter should include a mini-synopsis describing the project in more detail. Follow that with a short bio that emphasizes your writing credentials. The query should also explain why the book is likely to sell in today's marketplace, and tell the agent as much about your ability to write as it does about your book.

Here's an example of a winning *fiction* query letter, by Lynn Flewelling. This query, reprinted with permission, sold several agents on the book and ultimately won Flewelling a two-book deal with Bantam.

> Specific person
>
> Agency
>
> Address
>
> Dear (Agent/Editor's Name):
>
> I am seeking representation for my fantasy adventure novel, *Luck in the Shadows*, complete at 170,000 words. I am enclosing a synopsis and a sample chapter. The sequel, *Stalking Darkness*, is nearing completion and another free-standing book featuring the same characters is in outline form.
>
> I love thieves and spies—those sneaky people who live by intuition, skill, and inside knowledge. In fantasy, however, they are often portrayed as dark, ruthless characters or relegated to second string roles, a la Falstaff, as useful or amusing foils for more conventional heroic types. *Luck in the Shadows* gives the rogues center stage.
>
> Seregil is an experienced spy for hire with a murky past and noble connections; Alec is the talented but unworldly boy he rescues and takes on as apprentice. "I admit I've cut a purse or two in my time," Seregil tells Alec soon after they meet, "and some of what I do could be called stealing, depending on who you ask. But try to imagine the challenge of overcoming incredible obstacles to accomplish a noble purpose. Think of traveling to lands where legends walk the streets in daylight

and even the color of the sea is like nothing you've ever seen! I ask you again, would you be plain Alec of Kerry all your life, or would you see what lies beyond?" Alec goes, of course, and quickly plunges into danger, intrigue, and adventure as their relationship deepens into friendship. The interaction between these two forms the core of this character-driven series.

I've been writing professionally for ten years and am currently a freelance journalist. My articles appear regularly in the *Bangor Daily News*, *Preview! Magazine*, and *Maine in Print*. I've covered everything from software to psychics; my interview credits include Stephen King, Anne Rice, and William Kotzwinkle. Thank you for your consideration of this proposal. I look forward to hearing from you soon.

Sincerely,

Lynn Flewelling

And the following is an example of a successful *nonfiction* query letter, written by Karen Telleen-Lawton, which she sent by e-mail to Elizabeth Trupin-Pulli, an agent based in Santa Fe, New Mexico. (Also reprinted with permission.)

Date: Thursday, November 07

Dear Ms. Trupin-Pulli,

Drawing on Oaks (A Philosophy for Life Beyond Kids) is a perspective on emptying the nest and rediscovering life. I examine issues including personal and career midlife crises, relating to college children, and marriage in the long run, writing with humor and hope through the eclectic filters that define my worldview.

As an amateur naturalist and eco-gardener, I look to nature as a model. My economist's frame considers how people make everyday choices among scarce resources like time. As an engineer, I pick things apart to understand them, and my role as a mother tries to make them whole again. As a spiritual person, I filter events with an eye towards hope and forgiveness.

Short excerpts of my book have been published as essays and articles in magazines, newspapers, and a *Family Fun* magazine cookbook over the past half dozen years or so. *Draw-*

ing on Oaks pieces have enjoyed an excellent reception not only among their intended baby boomer market, but among younger and older audiences who either look forward to or reminisce on these days. I believe this inspirational memoir could draw a large share from this large market.

I would be pleased to send you further information. Thank you for your time.

Sincerely yours,

Karen Telleen-Lawton

A query letter is a calling card as much as a request for representation. Do you have more projects in you? If so, say so. Agents look for writers they can represent over the long term, and you should look for an agent with that in mind as well.

I recommend that you make a list of at least twenty potential agents. Make sure you have the specifics on how they want to be queried. Most agents today prefer an e-mail query. Don't call unless they specifically say to do so in their submission guidelines. Agents are always looking for fresh and talented new writers, but they are also very busy and most would be annoyed by a phone call. You don't want to annoy an agent before you've even queried him or her.

One other tip: If it's nonfiction, include the book proposal with the query. As Stephen Blake Mettee says in his book, *The Fast-Track Course on How to Write a Nonfiction Book Proposal*, if the agent or editor is wavering after reading the query, having the proposal readily available means they can look it over then and there. It's one more opportunity to impress them while you have their attention.

You should send out your queries in waves, say in bursts of five agents at a time. That way you can take advantage of any comments or suggestions you might receive from them along the way before querying the next wave.

Follow all submission guidelines for each individual agent you query, with perhaps one exception. There are differing views on this, but I believe simultaneous submissions to a number of agents is fine. In today's world, it's unreasonable to expect a writer to submit to one agent and then wait two to six months for a response. Even if they say "no simultaneous submissions," in the guidelines, you're better off ignoring that. If you have the tremendous good fortune of attracting more than one agent who is seriously interested in representing you, then you have the best of all worlds: a choice. You may need to smooth over some ruffled feathers, but chancing this beats wasting months or years waiting for agent after agent to respond. Be tactful, always.

Once you're offered representation, then what? What, exactly, does an agent do? Essentially, they get you a book contract with a publisher. They also will sell any subsidiary rights, like foreign market publication, electronic and audiobook rights, paperback rights, and sometimes movie rights. They'll negotiate an advance for you, make sure the contract you sign is as advantageous to you as possible, and be the intermediary between you and the publisher on all matters. If a dispute arises, the agent's job is to resolve it. They'll also protect your interests in any business or publishing decision. For example, if a magazine wants to excerpt a portion of your forthcoming book, your agent will negotiate the price the magazine will pay to do that.

> Most agents today prefer an e-mail query. Don't call unless they specifically say to do so in their submission guidelines.

"In addition to being a negotiator and career builder, the agent will become the 'content manager' for the author, overseeing the numerous channels into which a book can be placed and/or reshaped," agent Doris Booth explains.

For these services, plus many others, your agent will get a percentage of all your book income, including your advance, additional royalties, and subsidiary rights revenue. Typically, agents receive 10 percent to 15 percent of everything your book earns, which, given what a good agent does, is a bargain.

If at some point you decide you want a different agent, you can find another. Not all author/agent relationships work out. But any books you did with the first agent remain there, and you are obligated to pay that agent a percentage of any future earnings from those projects.

ADVANCES

Except for best-selling writers and celebrities, the days of big advances for writers are probably numbered.

The "entrepreneurial publisher" model, whereby the author gets little or no advance but a greater share in the profits, is starting to take hold among some of the larger presses. HarperCollins was the first of the big houses to try it in 2008. Its imprint, HarperStudio, blazed the trail with twenty-five authors who agreed to forgo large advances in exchange for 50 percent of their books' eventual profits. (Note: As this book went to press, HarperCollins announced that it planned to shutter HarperStudio and distribute its titles to the parent company's other imprints. It remains to be seen whether they will continue to offer the lower advances and higher royalties that HarperStudio became known for.)

"The profit-sharing plan, such as the one offered selectively by HarperCollins, has a lot of merit these days, especially for authors who already have a fairly good sales record," Booth says. But, she warns, be careful with whom you profit share: "There's a big difference between profit-sharing with HarperCollins and 'profit-sharing' with the vanity publisher who markets under the guise of being your 'partner.' "

Traditionally, publishers have paid advances to writers to compensate them for the time it would take to write and deliver a manuscript. While established writers can sometimes demand huge advances, say, in the hundreds of thousands of dollars, or even millions, most new writers are lucky to win a $5,000 or $10,000 advance. Smaller houses offer even lesser amounts. The theory, though, is that the publisher will not only make back the advance money once the book is published, but that both the publisher and the writer will benefit from any profits made in excess of the advance amount. For writers, that money arrives in the form of royalties, which are payments made based on a percentage of book sales.

So, as an example, a writer sells a book to a publisher and gets a $5,000 advance with the promise of royalties based on a certain percentage of the cover price for each book sold. If the royalty percentage is 10 percent of the cover price and the book retails for $24.95, the author would make about $2.50 per book. Once the book has earned back the $5,000, the writer starts to receive royalty checks. Let's say that, over time, there are 10,000 hardcover books sold. The total income the writer earns from these sales is $25,000, a figure which includes the $5,000 advance.

> While established writers can sometimes demand huge advances, say, in the hundreds of thousands of dollars, or even millions, most new writers are lucky to win a $5,000 or $10,000 advance.

Given that the writer has probably spent the better part of a year or more to write the book, the return on investment is fairly small. Of course, fiction writers who do well with their first books can demand larger advances, and, if their books continue to sell well, make more money over time. That's why writers depend on their books staying in print. The more books you have out there working for you, the more money you'll make.

Now, be aware that there are many variables with this formula. Percentages offered vary, and contracts can stipulate differing ways to calculate what's due. For example, the royalty can be based on the wholesale price of the book rather than the cover price. Most books are sold by a publisher to other booksellers at a discount of anywhere from 40 percent to 55 percent off the cover price. This means (continuing the previous example of the $24.95 retail price), with a 10 percent royalty rate on the wholesale price, the author would earn somewhere in the area of $1.12 to $1.50 per book sold.

Also, some contracts have tiered royalty rates. For example, you might earn 8 percent on the first 25,000 books sold, and 10 percent on the next 25,000. It can get complicated. The key is to have an agent who can get you the very best deal and explain it to you to your satisfaction.

This payment model has been in place for a long time, and it's likely to remain popular. But publishers are realizing they can no longer pay large advances on books that don't sell.

"The general principle stands that publishers and authors need to develop different ways of working in which they share the risks and rewards equitably," says publisher David Cole. Cole's company, Bay Tree Publishing, is a small press that publishes primarily nonfiction. The company's imprint, Ardenwood, offers copublishing (subsidized publishing) services as well.

"The days of a writer being a writer and a publisher taking the financial risk and doing all the marketing are over," he adds.

"I'd love to see publishing move in the direction of profit sharing," agent Laurie Abkemeier says. "Unfortunately, too many authors and agents are more concerned with what they can get upfront. We've learned to equate advance with love, when we should be most concerned with the right publishing fit. It's an uphill battle to retrain our thinking, but money has become a corrupting influence in publishing. Readers don't care how much someone was paid; they just want a great book. Deliver that, and the money will follow."

COPYRIGHT DO'S AND DON'TS

Anything you write—any work that is the product of your imagination or intellect—is protected by federal law. That includes any original work of authorship, such as a poem, play, novel, or magazine article. It also applies to other creative works like photography and graphic books. Copyright doesn't apply to the idea underlying the work, only the particular expression of the idea that you create. Likewise, facts are not protected by copyright, but the manner in which those facts are presented by an author is protected.

As the owner of the copyright, you have the right to sell or transfer those rights as you see fit. As a writer, you retain all rights to your writing with the exception of works made for hire, whereby someone pays you to produce the work under contract. In that case, the copyright rests with the entity that hired you. As an example, reporters who are employed by newspapers do not enjoy copyright over the work they produce for the newspaper. The copyright rests with the newspaper.

All original intellectual or artistic expressions are automatically protected upon creation. Also, any work created after March 1, 1989, does not require a notice of copyright (the small "c" in a circle), though in some instances it's advised to include it. For example, if you are self-publishing, you should include the symbol, which strengthens any action you might pursue against an infringement. Also, you do not have to register a work with the federal Copyright Office to be protected. One caveat: If you choose to sue someone for infringement, the work must first be registered. If registration is made within three months of publication of the work, the owner retains the right to sue for and collect attorneys' fee as well as some specific statutory damage amounts.

If your book, or other writing, is being printed by an established publisher or a periodical like a magazine, that entity will provide notice of copyright for your work. However, if you are simply sending your work to an agent or publisher for consideration, the symbol is unnecessary, and in some circles is considered the sign of an amateur.

> All original intellectual or artistic expressions are automatically protected upon creation.

Copyright is considered a "divisible" form of property, meaning that as the owner you can sell or transfer pieces of the work and any derivative works; for example, anything that draws upon the original work, like a screenplay, play, a video game, or even a condensed work (such as those found in *Reader's Digest*).

When you sell your book to a publisher, you are granting that publisher the primary right to publish the work in any and all forms, from hardcover to paperback to e-book. In addition, a publisher will almost surely want the rights to sell your book to foreign markets, produce book club or other special editions, and perhaps serialization rights for publishing the work in periodicals. Subsidiary, or secondary, rights usually mean selling the rights to derivative works like audio editions, motion picture and television rights, dramatic or performance rights, and merchandizing rights. All of these rights may be sold separately for additional compensation.

Think of J. K. Rowling's Harry Potter books. In addition to initial hardcover rights, she also benefited from the sale of trade and mass market paperback, audio and electronic rights, foreign market rights, film rights, and merchandising rights, just to name a few.

A writer's literary rights are at the heart of the proposed Google settlement with the Author's Guild and the American Publishers Association now in the courts. Part of the growing opposition to the settlement is authors' fear of losing their right to deny Google the ability to publish and distribute their books electronically. While the Author's Guild and the APA sought to reassure authors that they are acting in their best interests, many writers are not convinced.

"Google's [proposed] $125 million settlement with the Writers Guild and the Association of American Publishers will have a profound impact on every writer—one that has not begun to be assessed by the writing and publishing community," agent Doris Booth says. "The settlement [will set] in motion a tsunami of change in how royalties are figured and paid, and how content is distributed to readers. Every writer should study the settlement and understand its implications, as should every literary agent."

As of this writing, it remains to be seen how the Google issue will be resolved.

Your intellectual rights are sacrosanct. Never give them away and do not sell them without the advice of an agent or literary attorney. If you are negotiating directly with a publisher, know exactly which rights you are selling, and for how much. If you don't know, seek counsel.

5. Nonfiction Books: Opportunities Abound

"Writing is like prostitution. First you do it for love, and then for a few close friends, and then for money."—Moliere

The good news about nonfiction is if you are a good writer with a good idea—or several good ideas—you can make a living. You have more options and more opportunities than fiction writers. If you want to write nonfiction books, you can get a book contract on the strength of a well-written proposal, rather than having to have a complete manuscript. If you have expertise in a particular field, you already have the makings of a "platform," which everyone in publishing says you need (more on that in a minute). And while the newspaper industry seems to be in its death throes, it's still possible to write for print magazines, and for newspapers and magazines online.

As a nonfiction writer, you are in control. You choose what you want to write about, which publications to pitch, whether you want to write articles or books, and how often you want to write.

You also need to develop a platform. You'll see and hear that term frequently. Everyone seems to hate the word. But it's crucial to success, especially in nonfiction book writing. What it means, essentially, is your celebrity—what you're known for, or want to become known for, whether it is writing about pets (i.e. dog whisperer Cesar Millan), the domestic arts (Martha Stewart), politics (Michael

Moore), cooking (Rachael Ray), sports (Tiger Woods), or any other subject. If you are able to build recognition as an expert in a particular area, and can prove it with, say, the number of hits on your Web site or your followers on Twitter, or better yet, a robust seminar or lecture series, you've got a platform. If you are the person the media contacts when news breaks on your topic, all the better.

"Blog, get a column in your local newspaper or your favorite magazine, give a lecture series—it's the best thing nonfiction writers can do for themselves," says agent Victoria Skurnick. "Except for one thing: Have talent. I do not believe that talent will ever go completely unnoticed or unappreciated, midlist or no midlist."

Nonfiction writers, more than fiction writers, need to know how to market and promote their own work, because it's unlikely publishers are going to do it for you. The section on marketing in this book is full of ideas and suggestions, from using the Internet and e-mail to capitalizing on the latest in social networking tools to get the word out about your books or articles.

> What "platform" means, essentially, is your celebrity—what you're known for, or want to become known for.

The bottom line is, if you know how to write, have a ready-made audience—or know how to create one—and can write a query, you can be published. And, sometimes, a query will result in something unexpected, as it did with John Grogan.

Grogan was a columnist for the *Philadelphia Inquirer* when he sent an inquiry to nonfiction agent Laurie Abkemeier, hoping she might be interested in a collection of his columns. She wasn't. But tucked in neatly near the end of his letter were the words, "Already in progress is a first-person memoir, *Marley and Me*, about my life with a wildly neurotic Labrador retriever." Grogan also included a link to his column about Marley's death. It was touching and funny and beautifully written, but it turned out that was all there was to see, Abkemeier recalls. The memoir wasn't really "in progress" at all, merely "percolating." At Abkemeier's urging, Grogan began writing a chapter a week and sending it to her. After nearly nine months, the manuscript was complete and was sent out to editors.

That was the beginning of what would become a whirlwind of publishing success. *Marley and Me* debuted in November 2005 and quickly became an international best seller. It has since sold more than six million copies and has been made into a major motion picture, starring Owen Wilson and Jennifer Aniston (Fox, 2008). The early success sparked a best-selling line of children's books, including *Bad Dog, Marley!*; *A Very Marley Christmas*; and *Marley: A Dog Like No Other*. Grogan's second memoir, *The Longest Trip Home*, was published in 2008.

The moral of the story? Sometimes you don't know what's going to grab the attention of an agent or editor. Always be open to the possibility of serendipity.

Abkemeier says she has seen a wave of high-concept, often Internet-platform-based books in the past year.

"Five years ago, I could sell solid books with what I would characterize as fresh concepts, but editors have gotten more interested in the extreme and bizarre rather than just the quirky," she says. "With the rise of information easily accessible online, books need to have more personality than ever. That trend will continue. Reference and travel readers are finding what they need online, although there will always be room for the definitive books—like *What to Expect When You're Expecting*, and the single-subject travel guides that people want to take on their trips."

"In nonfiction, most books that get published, bought, and read are midlist (books that sell moderately and continuously). Large-advance books tend to lose money," agent Jeff Herman explains. "A stable backlist of midlist evergreens is what enables large houses to sustain themselves. That's not going to change, because it can't."

In fact, there is tremendous opportunity in nonfiction book writing. Many of the agents and editors I interviewed for this book told me they routinely read blogs and online magazines, looking for writers who are writing on topics that lend themselves to book treatment. If you are knowledgeable about a particular subject, you can probably turn that interest and expertise into a book idea. And the good thing is you can sell your idea on the strength of a sound proposal. Also, while it's good to have an agent, it's not required. I sold this book directly to the publisher.

"There are imprints, small and large, that will nurture good new authors," says Elfrieda Abbe, publisher of *The Writer* magazine. "Writers just have to find them. It takes time and research. Right now, writers of nonfiction have a better chance of getting published than fiction writers."

EllynAnne Geisel was writing a personal recollection about vintage aprons ten years ago and she suddenly considered how much history was woven into each one. Who wore it and when? What family memories existed in each apron string and pocket? She was so taken with the idea that she embarked on a four-year apron journey, collecting vintage aprons and writing down the apron memories of storytellers from all over America. She then wrote and curated a national traveling exhibit, "Apron Chronicles: A Patchwork of American Recollections." Ultimately, she wrote an award-winning book, *The Apron Book: Making, Wearing and Sharing a Bit of Cloth and Comfort*, a companion gift book, *Apronisms: Pocket Wisdom for Every Day*, and *The Kitchen Linens Book: Using, Sharing and Cherishing the Fabrics of Our Daily Lives*. The point is, EllynAnne turned a simple diary entry into a successful book franchise.

Jerry Camarillo Dunn Jr., who teaches travel writing at SBWC, took a question that many people asked him in his career as a travel writer and turned it around to come up with a great book idea. Since he has traveled so widely, people constantly ask him, "What is your favorite place?" So he decided to ask celebrities and other well-known people the same question. The result is *My Favorite Place on Earth: Celebrated People Share Their Travel Discoveries*, published by National Geographic in 2009. Dunn interviewed such diverse personalities as Sandra Day O'Connor and the Dalai Lama, actors Robin Williams and Morgan Freeman, astronauts Buzz Aldrin and Sally Ride, explorer Jean-Michel Cousteau, real estate mogul Donald Trump, entertainer Jerry Seinfeld, food guru Alice Waters, and author Tony Hillerman. Each one told Dunn about his or her "favorite place on Earth," ranging from the San Francisco Bay area to Bali.

> "There are imprints, small and large, that will nurture good new authors. Writers just have to find them. It takes time and research. Right now, writers of nonfiction have a better chance of getting published than fiction writers."
> —publisher Elfrieda Abbe

Say you're a sports writer and you have a good relationship with a well-known ball player you've been covering for some years. Why not do a book on him? You could come up with any number of ideas: on his philosophy on life, his early childhood, or how his parents or an early coach influenced him.

Or, if you write about restaurants, maybe there is a book based on the compiling of information about the best family-friendly restaurants in New Orleans. Maybe Los Angeles needs a book on the best Thai restaurants, or the best restaurants with nightlife.

Food writers have unlimited opportunities. One of the more inventive examples in recent years is *Julie & Julia*, a memoir by Julie Powell, who attempted to revitalize her marriage, restore her ambition, and save her soul by cooking all five-hundred and twenty-four recipes in Julia Child's *Mastering the Art of French Cooking, Volume I*, over the course of one year. Powell's book became a bestseller, and it was also was made into a major motion picture starring Meryl Streep.

If you're an outdoor writer, consider adventure books: the best hiking trails in Maui, best biking in the Rockies, or best snowboarding spots in Canada. The possibilities are unlimited.

Mitch Albom was a Detroit sports writer who wrote a memoir about visits with his old sociology professor as the professor was dying of Lou Gehrig's disease in 1995. The book, *Tuesdays with Morrie*, became a huge bestseller and Albom has since written several more.

Los Angeles Times columnist Steve Lopez turned a series of columns into a best-selling book about a former Julliard student whose mental illness destroyed his career as a cello player. Lopez met Nathaniel Ayers on Skid Row and befriended him over time. He introduced him to other musicians and ultimately helped convince Ayers to move into an apartment and off the streets. Lopez's book, *The Soloist*, came out in 2008 and was made into a major motion picture the following year.

Abkemeier says every writer is different and every book is different. There is no formula for success:

> But you do need to have some sort of platform, some sort of relevant background. I get queries all the time from people who say, "My qualification is that I'm just a normal person." Seriously. And it's ridiculous. Agents and publishers are looking for standout individuals, people who are impressive and unique, with backgrounds that match their subjects.
>
> If you've ever had to hire someone and you've looked through dozens or even hundreds of resumes, you know what I mean. Most people all look the same, but there are a handful who stand out. Agents and publishers are looking for those same qualities that make us take notice. I'd say the single biggest factor for me, however, is writing voice. If I make an instant connection with the writer, I'm more likely to ask to see the material even if it's not something I would normally think I'd be interested in.

Do you have expertise in a specific area? Is there someone or something you have returned to in your writing over time? An organization or a person who is extraordinary? Have you had extraordinary experiences of your own that might be turned into a memoir?

"If you have something to say, and have a compelling desire to share those thoughts, then write, write, write," author and editor Diane Gedymin says. "But authors today don't have the luxury of living in a vacuum. They must read, read, read and research, research, research to make sure their book idea is unique and viable in the marketplace."

Once you have an idea, you need to write a book proposal. There are a number of excellent guides, including *The Fast-Track Course on How to Write a Nonfiction Book Proposal*, by Stephen Blake Mettee. Published by Quill Driver Books, Mettee's guide includes everything you need to know about how to write a query letter and a book proposal. It also includes tips on dealing with agents and publishers, a sample query letter, a sample proposal, and an example of a typical book contract.

> Do you have expertise in a particular area? Is there someone or something you have returned to in your writing over time? Have you had extraordinary experiences of your own that might be turned into a memoir?

Jeff Herman also has an excellent book, written with his wife, Deborah Levine Herman, called *Write the Perfect Book Proposal: 10 That Sold and Why*. It highlights ten successful proposals and details what worked and what didn't in each case.

I also recommend Michael Larsen's guide, *How to Write a Book Proposal*. Larsen is an agent with Larsen-Pomada Literary Agency in San Francisco, and the latest edition of his book has much information about today's publishing world and tips for finding just the right publisher for your project. Larsen's book also has sample book proposals, with notes and annotations to show what the authors did right and what they did wrong.

A good book proposal will describe the project, explain who the author is and why the author is the only person who can write the book, include a market analysis and promotion plan, a chapter outline and at least one sample chapter. Typically, a book proposal will be between thirty and sixty pages.

When you're writing your proposal, consider other projects that could be successful offshoots. Does the book lend itself to a sequel or even a series? What about a movie tie-in, for example a documentary? What merchandising opportunities are there? Clothing, canvas bags, mugs, toys?

In the end, creating a career in nonfiction book writing isn't easy, but the opportunities are greater than with fiction writing.

Herman advises: "Keep your eyes on the money, which means keep your eyes on the people who buy the products, and accommodate them first and last, because the people who spend the money are never wrong, even if we don't like their choices. Everything else is secondary. Generate what people will pay for, and figure out how to let them know that they want it enough to pay for it, and don't stop or look backward."

6. Should You Self-Publish?

"You can't wait for inspiration, you have to go after it with a club."
—*Jack London*

For years, self-published books have suffered from an industry bias—in many ways justified—that such books would never see the light of day with a "legitimate" publisher. In the past, they have typically suffered from bad writing and editing, adding to the belief that a self-published book is inferior to that published by a traditional publisher. As author N. Frank Daniels says, "Those days are long gone."

"More and more, given the lack of traditional opportunities, authors are self-publishing with great success," says Diane Gedymin, former executive editorial director of Author Solutions, which is now the parent company of iUniverse, AuthorHouse, Xlibris, and other publishing service providers. "In the fiction categories, quality is essential, but there are unknown writers who have written fine books. Authors who are committed to their individual success can continue to publish and promote their books with the hopes of reaching as many readers as possible."

Now a book editor and publishing consultant, Gedymin is also coauthor with Susan Driscoll of *Get Published! Professionally, Affordably, Fast*, published through iUniverse.

"What's different now is that self-published books are no longer stigmatized and the number of published titles has thus soared," she adds, while advising:

"If an author truly has a fabulous book and an even better platform, that author should try to get represented and published in the traditional way, whether it's a mainstream agent/publisher route or a smaller press. Still, self-publishing is now an option for any author, but the rules of success still apply. An amateurish book—both inside and out—will not be able to compete against the big-time publishers."

When your book is accepted by a traditional publisher, the publishing house provides certain services, including editing, cover and content design, production, distribution to booksellers, and some—often minimal—level of promotion. The publisher not only usually pays you an advance of some amount, but also assumes all the costs of editing, designing, producing, and distributing the book, as well as spending money marketing it. As the author, in this scenario, you are paid royalties. All other profits go to the publisher.

Fiction writers should first exhaust all efforts to get an agent and win a traditional publishing contract before looking into self-publishing—for two reasons. The first is self-publishing makes much more sense for a nonfiction title that has a particular niche and whose author has the wherewithal and the ability to spend a lot of time marketing it. The second is, while there are notable exceptions, there is still a lot of industry bias against self-published novels. However, if all your efforts at selling the book to a traditional publisher fail, then by all means consider self-publishing. It's very possible you will attract the attention of a larger publisher if your self-published book takes off.

"On self-publication for fiction, anything that eases the way for writing to reach readers is good," editor David Ebershoff says. "If the writing holds up, that's good. I'm never surprised when self-publication leads to a more traditional book contract."

If you self-publish, whether fiction or nonfiction, be careful with whom you do business. Be especially wary of the online publishers which have, for the most part, replaced what used to be known as vanity presses. Rarely, publishers share in the costs, or they publish based on receiving a percentage of profits, in which case they usually are selective about which projects they take on. There are lots of horror stories out there, so look before you leap.

> "What's different now is that self-published books are no longer stigmatized and the number of published titles has thus soared."
>
> —editor Diane Gedymin

Unless you have a good understanding of the entire process of book production and can do your own marketing, self-publishing probably isn't for you. But, particularly if you have a nonfiction book project and already have some publishing savvy—or are willing to put a lot of time into learning—self-publishing may be a wise choice.

With those caveats, let's take a look at some of the ways you can self-publish your book.

ONLINE "PUBLISHERS"

The newer print-on-demand companies that operate online and often refer to themselves as publishers, such as iUniverse and Lulu. com, offer most of the services of a traditional publisher, either on an a la carte basis or in packages for which you pay a fee. Your book will be printed using print-on-demand (POD) technology. POD allows one book at a time to be produced. The quality isn't the same as with an offset printing process, but it is improving every day. These companies offer services ranging from acquiring an ISBN (International Standard Book Number) for your book, editing the manuscript, designing the cover, typesetting the book, and arranging to have it printed, as well as production of e-book versions and distribution to bookstores (primarily online stores), along with minimal marketing.

In fall 2009, Lulu offered book service packages ranging from $369 to $1,369. iUniverse offered similar services ranging from $599 to $2,099. These are base fees, and once you add up all the various services to produce and market a book, plus pay for the number of books you want to have on hand, the total cost can run into many thousands of dollars.

One major advantage of print-on-demand is, since you can produce one book at a time, there's no need to print and store a large stock of books. Each book can be printed as it's ordered online. The other, probably most important, feature is you keep all profits, less the fees paid to the self-publishing company. But remember, those fees can add up quickly if you're not sure what services you want or need.

One expense to keep in mind is the cost to produce however many initial copies you'll want for marketing. iUniverse's top packages provide twenty trade paperback copies, but only one hardcover copy. (A trade paperback is a softcover book that is larger and of a higher-quality than mass-market paperbacks, which are the paperbacks you typically see in supermarkets and drugstores.) If you want one hundred books for marketing purposes, you'll likely pay the full cost to produce any beyond those provided with the package.

Distribution also is a major issue for most people who self-publish. iUniverse says it will offer your book on its own Web site, but it also offers, for an additional fee, the option of having it distributed through two other major book wholesalers—Baker & Taylor and Ingram Book Company (via a POD division of Ingram named Lightning Source). Distribution through those two companies means it would be available on Barnes & Noble's Web site and Amazon.com.

Most of these online companies charge extra fees for distribution beyond their Web sites and offer nonstandard discounts and terms that have a chilling effect on sales to retailers, so beware.

There are some people who believe using an online POD company is a huge mistake.

Ken Atchity, whose company, Atchity Entertainment International, Inc., packages books and film deals, says:

> One major advantage of print-on-demand is, since you can produce one book at a time, there's no need to print and store a large stock of books.

Self-publishing is now widely referred to as "entrepreneurial publishing" (a term that stands for all publishing that is not "traditional," in the sense where the only one investing actual money in the publication is the publisher). It will continue, grow, and become even more important than it is already. But imprinted print-on-demand, I hope, will evaporate from the face of the Earth.

Writers have no idea what kind of damage it does to their credibility to publish through POD "publishers" (like iUniverse). For one thing, it almost certainly eliminates their being taken seriously by the entertainment media, who know full well the names of the POD publishers and have the attitude that the POD-published writer has (a) decided to pay for his publication and (b) doesn't have the enterprise to do it professionally.

SUBSIDY PUBLISHING

Ernie Witham (erniesworld.com), who teaches humor writing at SBWC, has been writing a humor column for newspapers for more than ten years and is anthologized in a number of *Chicken Soup for the Soul* books. Witham just published his second collection of stories based on his columns using Fithian Press (danielpublishing.com/fpmonth.htm), a quality subsidy press owned by another longtime SBWC workshop leader, John Daniel. Daniel describes Fithian as a small-press copublisher. Under a typical copublisher agreement, the author pays all the major production costs, including typesetting, printing, and binding. The publisher provides editorial services like editing, proofreading, and jacket copy; production services like design and typesetting; marketing services like press releases, brochures, sending out review copies, sales, and fulfillment; and distribution to bookstores and online retailers. The print run is typically short, in the 500 to 2,000 copy range. All copies are the property of the author, who receives a royalty of 60 percent of all net receipts on book and subsidiary rights sales.

If you are paying attention, you'll quickly realize that this rarely turns out to be a money-making venture for the author. So, as Daniel advises on his Web site, you have to have a very good reason to see your book in print. This is true in all self-publishing situations, by the way.

Why, exactly, do you want your book published? Do you seek attention? Do you want to use the book to support other work, like speaking? Is it because you want to leave a family history for your children and grandchildren? Perhaps you're tired of banging your head against the traditional publishers' doors and you have a well-thought-out plan for promotion and marketing. Or, you may have expertise in a field that is too narrow for a larger publisher to consider; how to repair clocks, for example.

Witham wanted to publish the collections for his many fans, but he also wanted to establish credibility as a humor-writing teacher. His first book, called *Ernie's World: The Book*, featured columns he writes for the *Montecito Journal*, a community newspaper published near Santa Barbara, California. Having a book also means he can market himself as an author, not just a columnist or a contributing writer. It helps in marketing his work, and it got him invited to be a presenter at several other writers conferences. It also opened the door for him to write for several magazines.

"Because I write about everyday family experiences, which a lot of columnists do, it is also a family history of sorts," Witham says.

It's worth noting that Ernie is a professional photographer and does magazine production for a living, so he has a lot of knowledge about the publication process. He had one thousand copies of *Ernie's World: The Book* published, and he sold about three-quarters of them before he started thinking about doing another book. Witham says there was a Los Angeles-based publisher who initially expressed interest in the first book. However, the publisher wanted not just a collection of columns, but a humor book with a theme; for example, a funny book on computers, or hiking. So Ernie went with Fithian. When he decided to do a second book, he based it on the theme of writing. *A Year in the Life of a "Working" Writer: A Memoir to the Best of the Recollection of Ernie Witham* came out in fall 2009. That's a great title, by the way. Witham also got some of the better-known authors he had met at the Santa Barbara Writers Conference to give him blurbs and write a terrific foreword for the book, which is selling well. Will Witham make money with it? He hopes so. However, the key is having a good reason to self-publish and a strategy for using the book beyond simply publishing it and hoping people will buy it.

> "Because I write about everyday family experiences, which a lot of columnists do, my book is also a family history of sorts."
>
> —author Ernie Witham

"Self-publishing is more acceptable than ever as an option but much more difficult to bring off well," Bay Tree Publishing Co. owner David Cole explains. "We are currently working with authors in a variety of copublishing arrangements that emphasize our expertise in editing, design, and distribution, while relying on authors for a greater commitment to marketing their own works. For an enthusiastic author with all but a blockbuster book, such arrangements can be very advantageous."

If you decide to use one of the subsidy self-publishers, it would be worth your while to get a copy of Mark Levine's *The Fine Print of Self-Publishing*. The book compares forty-five self-publishing companies, from online services like iUniverse and Lulu to lesser-known presses like Cold Water Press, Dog Ear, and Wordclay. This book tells you what to look for in a self-publisher, explains contracts, and pinpoints specific companies you should avoid.

"Entrepreneurial publishing at its best has high professional standards—witness the books of Greenleaf Publishing Group or Five Star Publications," Atchity says. "In our experience there is little or no onus on books that are published in this fashion when it comes to their future distribution by major traditional publishers or their potential for film or television. If you're doing POD, do it yourself! I'm all for small indie publishing, but in this situation a writer loses the same control he'd lose with a traditional house, and receives nothing or almost nothing up front. My advice is to proceed with caution and weigh carefully whether small indie is better than entrepreneurial publishing. In some cases, it might well be—for example, if your publisher is a prestigious one. In some cases, you'd be better off doing it yourself."

TRADITIONAL SELF-PUBLISHING

Before online POD publishers appeared, self-publishing truly meant the author published the book on his or her own, from typesetting to arranging for printing and distribution.

Starshine Roshell, a California newspaper columnist, self-published a collection of her columns in 2008 entitled, *Keep Your Skirt On: Kicky Columns With Legs*. Her columns are funny observations of her life as a wife and working mother of two young boys in suburban America. Her husband, John Roshell, is a book and Web designer who co-founded Comicraft, which publishes comic books and graphic novels. So John was able to design and produce the book, and he had the skill and knowledge necessary to contract with a print-on-demand printer. The initial print run was one thousand books.

The Roshells launched the book with a big party at a local art gallery, served boutique cupcakes and wine, and invited everyone in town. The highlight of the night was Starshine, who got up and told some hilarious stories from the book. She told me later they sold enough books that night to cover all their up-front publishing costs. (All the expenses for the party were donated. How cool is that?)

Then, a friend in show business in Los Angeles gave the book to someone who knows someone in Hollywood, and soon Starshine's book was being talked about as the basis of a new television series. Kind of like a "Sex in the City" for suburbia. If the TV show never comes to be, the book itself has been a great success. Every book ordered now is printed on demand and the profit goes directly to the bottom line.

This kind of self-publishing is not for the faint of heart. If you have the experience and knowledge, as Starshine and John Roshell did, go for it. But first, I recommend you read several books.

In addition to Dan Poynter's *The Self-Publishing Manual*, you should become familiar with Morris Rosenthal's *Print-on-Demand Book Publishing: A New Approach to Printing and Marketing Books for Publishers and Self-Publishing Authors* (fonerbooks.com), as well as Aaron Shepard's two titles, *Aiming at Amazon: The NEW Business of Self-Publishing* and *How to Publish Your Books with Print on Demand and Online Book Marketing on Amazon.com* (newselfpublishing.com).

Aiming at Amazon explains in great detail how to produce your book. The focus is on Amazon because, as Shepard explains, that is the most efficient and most lucrative way to distribute a self-published book.

Rosenthal's book, *Print-on-Demand Book Publishing*, provides detailed information on the process of print-on-demand publishing and explains how someone with savvy can make a decent living publishing his or her own books.

"Informational writers (how-to, self help, etc.) will continue to experiment with self-publishing, e-books, and publishing online. The number of books published outside the large trade system may continue to grow, thanks to on-demand printing, but I wouldn't be surprised if the larger trades cut back on the number of titles published, as they cut staff and the book superstore chains struggle," Rosenthal says. He goes on to report:

"With the advent of print-on-demand, the number of books published is no longer an important metric in judging the health of the publishing industry. I would be surprised if the average sales for 80 percent of books 'published' today was more than a few dozen copies, especially if you eliminate family and friends from the sales count."

Rosenthal says the main transition going on today in the non-literary book market is the move to the Internet, where the same content that would have been published as a book a few years ago may now be given away for free, in return for advertising revenue or sales of paper copies to people who would like to own the book or give it as a gift:

"This is mainly happening in the self-publishing community, as the larger trades see giving away content as a direct threat to their business models, and have so far entirely missed the Internet boat."

So, how can a writer position himself for self-publishing?

"By adopting that worst of all trade publishing catch-phrases: Build a platform," Rosenthal says.

Nothing is more important for writers today than the ability to market their own work, he says, and that's just as true for the trade-published author as for the self-publisher:

> Of course, it's easy to say, "Go out and become famous and then write a book," but the logic isn't that far from the truth. I can't tell you how many authors write me for advice about

publishing their memoirs, with the theory that as soon as people read about their uniquely exciting lives, they'll become famous and the book will attain best-seller status. Of course, the opposite is true, and the memoir market is driven by the life stories of famous people.

Fame aside, credentials help for non-literary books, being a somebody in the field, teaching the subject at a university, or better still, being a public "expert" who gets speaking gigs at conferences and media exposure.

Short of that, the best way for non-literary writers to build a platform is to create their own Web site, and build it around their writing, Rosenthal says. The site has to have compelling content that will attract readers and links, with a large quantity of free writing, ideally organized as a resource. (See Chapter 9.)

> "Nothing is more important for writers today than the ability to market their own work, and that's just as true for the trade-published author as for the self-publisher."
> —publisher Morris Rosenthal

"The same material that gets posted to the Web site can be used in books, providing they are on the same subject, and it's a terrific way for the writer to draw feedback on the work and to get a feel for the size of the marketplace," he adds.

Rosenthal advises: Become an expert. "Name recognition just isn't a practical goal in any niche market, and as soon as you get outside of the small circle of bestsellers each year, all book markets are niche markets."

Diversify your writing income.

"As a self-publisher using print-on-demand, I manage my backlist revisions and updates in accordance with the market, as opposed to rushing out new editions on an arbitrary schedule, and I publish my own e-books as well. By selling e-books direct from my own Web site, I've created a substantial source of income that is independent of both Amazon and my printer (Lightning Source), though I still need the search engines to send visitors to my site. As long as my fonerbooks.com Web site is drawing a couple of million visitors a year, I should be able to make a living from writing one way or another," Rosenthal explains.

7. Freelancing for Magazine and Online Publications

"Some editors are failed writers, but so are most writers."—T. S. Eliot

More writers are looking for freelance work these days, so the competition is stiff for jobs writing for print magazines. Even so, niche magazines—travel, computing, gardening, science, education, gourmet food, whatever you subscribe to at home —all offer a potential freelance gig.

Some airline magazines rely on freelancers for up to 95 percent of their content, according to Ty Treadwell (tytreadwell.com), who wrote about the in-flight magazine market for *The Writer* in January 2009. Among his many tips: Become familiar with the magazine to which you plan to pitch stories; be aware of the various destinations the airline serves; suggest ideas for the magazine's "front of the book" section, which offers more opportunities for new freelancers; and finally, be aware of the kinds of stories airline magazines aren't interested in (air disaster stories being one obvious example).

"The biggest no-no of all…is to propose an article that reflects negatively on any aspect of the airline industry," Treadwell says.

This is good advice that extends to any niche market. Use your common sense. If you're pitching stories to travel magazines, it's probably best to stay away from, say, an article about how bad the bedbug infestation is in foreign hotels. If you're suggesting pieces to food magazines, a long piece on the incidence of Montezuma's revenge in Mexico is not advisable.

Other niche magazines to consider include those that focus on pets and show animals (cats, dogs, birds); horses; specialty crafts like knitting or crochet; vintage crafts; farming and agriculture; home repair and improvement; real estate; education; every kind of sport; and almost all trades.

Once you decide what you want to write, familiarize yourself with the magazines that specialize in that topic. Start with local and regional magazines, because the opportunities are generally greater closer to home. Read at least six months of past issues, and then get the magazine's submission guidelines. Most magazines post them on their Web sites, or you can send a SASE to the editorial office requesting the publication's guidelines.

Once you are familiar with the publication, send the editor a query by e-mail, pitching three story ideas. Flesh them out enough to give the editor a good idea of how each story would be written. I recommend three because it improves your chances of piquing his or her interest with at least one of the ideas. Provide a link to your Web site where he or she can see work you've already written. (If you are

> Use your common sense. If you're pitching stories to travel magazines, it's probably best to stay away from, say, an article about how bad the bedbug infestation is in foreign hotels.

just starting out, offer to write something for a small publication for free so you'll have samples of your work.) Follow up if you don't hear back from the editor within two or three weeks. And keep sending story ideas every month or two. Eventually, you're likely to get an assignment. By the way, both *Writer's Digest* and *The Writer* magazines provide directories of freelance opportunities at the back of every issue, so it would be wise to subscribe to one or both of them for ideas.

Here is an example of a good query to a magazine editor that resulted in an assignment. Notice the detail the writer, Vukani G. Nyirenda, uses in the pitch (excerpt reprinted with permission from Margot Finke's "Musings" column in the *Purple Crayon*, "Query Letters That Worked," Part Two—underdown.org/mf-sample-query-letters.htm):

> July 20, 2006
>
> Fandangle Magazine
>
> C/O Nancy Cavanaugh
>
> 14 Schult Street
>
> Keene, NH 03431
>
> Dear Ms. Cavanaugh:
>
> How do American children born of multicultural, multiracial intermarriages feel about their identity? Do they accept who they are? Are they comfortable with their identity? Do they know who they are? These questions must be of concern to the many American children who find themselves in such situations.
>
> For your next issue of *Fandangle Magazine*, I propose to submit a story of about 600 words titled: "Who Am I?" In the story, a nine year old girl of multicultural intermarriage between an African man and an American lady is troubled by the question of her identity. But her parents dismiss her question simply. Her friends tease her about her name and identity. She turns to her African grandfather for an answer, but he is hard of hearing. When she discovers he can read English, she poses the question to him in a poem. The grandfather asks why she is concerned. In response she says, "I really, really, don't know who I am. My mom and my dad say they know who I am. But I don't. I mean, who am I?"
>
> Formerly a university lecturer, university administrator and civil servant in Zambia, Africa, I now live in California. I am a graduate of Long Ridge Writer's Group, Institute of Children's Literature and member of the Society of Children's Book Writers and Illustrators. My one children's story: "Too Clever by Half" has been published in an anthology titled, *The Gathering*

of the Minds, (San Francisco, doorwaytothemind.com). I could also write other children's stories with a Zambian (African) flavor if this meets with your needs.

I thank you for your time and look forward to hearing from you.

Yours sincerely,

Vukani G. Nyirenda

Michelle Theall, founder of *Women's Adventure* magazine, says print magazines are looking less for "service" pieces, those that offer basic information (how-tos and where-tos), because the Internet does that so well: "Publishers will need to supply readers with information or images that cannot easily be gotten or have the same impact as they would online." Theall remarks:

> Good talent is cheap right now. Even great writers are struggling to find work. Magazines are closing their doors, so there are fewer places to pitch work.
>
> Don't waste an editor's time. Rigorously study the magazine and pitch a fresh and unique angle. Most of the queries we get are of subjects we've covered a million times and a million different ways. Be relevant. Unique. And have the clips to back it up.
>
> It seems these days that there are more writers than readers, but that's not really the case. People are just changing the ways in which they receive content. But content still must be created. This means the writer needs to be versatile—able and willing to write for the Web, magazines, and video.

Many businesses have trade newsletters and hire freelancers to provide content. A quick Google search returned thousands of newsletters focusing on topics ranging from how to protect your privacy to using technology to drive traffic to your Web site to business tips for the self-employed.

Writing for Online Publications

Versatility is important, because newer technologies also offer new places to sell your writing. Online magazines, or e-zines, offer increasing opportunities. When online magazines first started to publish, the idea of getting paid to write for them was almost laughable. The best ones—*Slate* and *Salon* come to mind—paid some of their more well-known writers, but generally if you wrote for an online publication you pretty much did it for the experience. Fortunately, that's changed and today the more serious and respected online magazines are paying good money to their contributors. Even *The Huffington Post*, which depends for the most part on unpaid bloggers, has a stable of staff writers, and in early 2009 it reported it would spend $1.7 million to hire eight investigative reporters.

Miller-McCune Magazine is a good example of an online magazine that pays well. I do some freelancing for *Miller-McCune*, which focuses on academic research in the areas of education, politics, the environment, economics, urban affairs, and health. The aim is to influence policymakers and bring about innovative solutions to social problems. *Miller-McCune* pays a very decent rate, in fact better than some of the print magazines I write for.

Writing for online publication forces you to think differently about how you present information. Because you have the ability to hyperlink to any online source, you can use that technique to provide explanatory and background information and save space for the actual news of the story you're writing. So, for example, if I'm writing about schizophrenia, I can hyperlink to a medical or advocacy site that provides all the information one would need on the disease rather than spend two or three sentences repeating a boilerplate definition. *Miller-McCune* online not only publishes news about cutting-edge research, but also features a blog written by its staff and other writers.

Miller-McCune's online editor, Michael Todd, says:

> In publishing as a whole, I expect to see large numbers of
> skilled journalists being dumped on the market, trying to

re-invent themselves as "writers." While not all will succeed, the competition will intensify problems created by the reduction in outlets for well-paid writing. The Web and its offspring will continue to provide more and more forums for the written word, but the ability to make a living will require increased entrepreneurial acuity.

For my purposes I'd rather groom promising apprentice—or journeyman-level—writers. Beyond just the price break and reduction in the hassle factor, someone who hasn't commoditized him- or herself can bring a fresher perspective to their subject matter.

As a writer, how can you take advantage of these potential new markets? The first thing is to research the online magazine market. Also, look for traditional print magazines with online presences. Many, like *Miller-McCune*, publish the content from the print magazine but also offer fresh content, and that's where many writers can find work.

> "It seems these days that there are more writers than readers, but that's not really the case. People are just changing the ways in which they receive content."
>
> —editor Michelle Theall

Or, you can create your own online publication.

Jerry Roberts is a veteran newspaper reporter and editor who unexpectedly found himself unemployed in 2006 after a falling out with the owner of the *Santa Barbara News-Press*. Roberts, who was executive editor at the time, and five other top editors and reporters, walked out when owner Wendy McCaw decided to insert herself into the day-to-day coverage of the local news. A former political reporter, editorial page editor, and managing editor of the *San Francisco Chronicle*, Roberts has since written a weekly political column for the *Santa Barbara Independent* and advises the campus newspaper at the University of California, Santa Barbara.

In early 2009, Roberts and longtime friend and onetime rival Phil Trounstine decided to launch a blog called Calbuzz, which has since become the go-to Web site for news, commentary, and analysis of California politics. As Roberts explains:

> Phil and I were friendly competitors back in the day, when he was political editor at the *San Jose Mercury-News* and I had the same position at the *Chronicle*, covering the 1990 governor's race (one of the last great times there was a large, vibrant political press corps) and the great political year of 1992 (the Clinton-Perot-Bush I race, plus the "Thelma and Louise" Senate races that elected Dianne Feinstein and Barbara Boxer).
>
> Early in 2009, we were talking by e-mail, bemoaning the fact that the Field Poll had just come out with a new survey that included Dianne Feinstein as a possible gubernatorial candidate. Both of us had looked at the race and felt quite certain, based on the facts, that there was no way she would run and were shaking our heads at a) the decimated ranks of true political reporters in the wake of the demise of newspapers and b) the way that those left were simply reporting the findings of the Field Poll without any analysis of the likelihood that it was distorted by one very major misassumption in putting it together.

Roberts says he and Trounstine had talked from time to time about working on a project together:

"So we quite casually talked each other into starting a political blog specifically to write about this issue and, from time to time, others to fill in what we saw as gaps in strong analysis in California reporting."

Their first blog, "Why Dianne Feinstein Won't Run for Governor," ran on the op-ed page of the *Los Angeles Times* that same day, with a reference to the Web site at the bottom of the piece. They also sent out an e-blast to about five hundred people from Roberts' and Trounstine's personal lists of newspaper and political contacts.

"The combination of print, Web, and e-mail marketing worked far better than we thought, and we got a much bigger reaction that we expected: six hundred unique visitors the first day, as I recall, but, more important, pick-ups, references, and links in other media," Roberts says.

"At the beginning, we were planning on posting only occasionally, a couple times a week at most, but as we did more stories, the clearer it became that there was a niche for the kind of stuff we did—well-reported analysis and commentary—and the stronger the feedback loop became."

Calbuzz had the first interview with Jerry Brown about running for California governor, an interview with state Assemblyman Abel Maldonado in which he disclosed that Republican legislators in their private meetings were openly discussing "driving the state off a cliff" financially to achieve their slash-government agenda, and the first big takeout on why California had become ungovernable and the reform movement that was growing up to do something about it.

Roberts reports: "The thing became self-perpetuating; as more people read it, we started to get tips and comments that led to more stories. Along about May, we decided to make a move from a blog to a full-blown Web site."

In June 2009, they launched the new site with a piece called "The Calbuzz Primary Starts Today," an analysis of the 2010 governor's race. Calbuzz started to become not only a distinct voice but also a player in the political dynamic from day to day and began to move into the category of "must read" for the California political cognoscenti.

> "The combination of print, Web and e-mail marketing worked far better than we thought, and we got a much bigger reaction that we expected."
>
> —Calbuzz co-founder Jerry Roberts

"To our surprise, within a couple of months, we were named—along with Flashreport and Calitics—as one of the top political sites in California by 'The Fix,' *The Washington Post's* insider Web column, which also raised our profile," Roberts says.

"At this point, we're not doing much marketing, because just doing the content is almost a full-time job, and because we've got kind of a word-of-mouth, if-we-build-it-they-will-come attitude."

He and Trounstine hope to boost readership and advertising in coming years, focusing their reporting on the governor's race and other campaigns.

"Despite our 10,000 percent increase in revenues in six months, it's still largely a labor of love and will remain so, I expect," Roberts explains. Still, he says it's a lot of fun and they are helping train new journalists, as well. Several college student journalists have become regular contributors.

Calbuzz and other online news and information sites that focus on a particular subject are likely to grow in popularity, just as niche print publications have proliferated over the years.

"Whether we get our content online or in print in the future, we need writers to produce it and editors to edit it," says Elfrieda Abbe of *The Writer* magazine. "Writers, more than ever, need to be aware of all the media outlets available to them and how they can use them, whether it's traditional publishing or the latest thing on the Web. Knowing how to use the latest technology, from cell phones to electronic readers to the Internet, to deliver content is a definite asset."

8. Marketing—It's Up to You

"If a writer wrote merely for his time, I would have to break my pen and throw it away."—Victor Hugo

In this time of dizzying technological development, writers have to be ready and willing to embrace the new, *and to engage in marketing.*

Agent Laurie Abkemeier says:

> Marketing has always been a publisher's biggest challenge. The same strategy doesn't work for every book, and after decades of bookselling, it's awfully frustrating to still be throwing spaghetti at the wall to see what sticks. It always comes down to word-of-mouth, but why that starts about some books and not others remains a bit of a mystery. Or, I should say, it's obvious why it happens with some books and not others, but there are also books where you would think it should happen—the book gets tons of publicity or fabulous reviews or something significant—and for whatever reason, it doesn't translate into sales. Oftentimes I think you can trace it to a category issue, but not always.
>
> I hope that in the next few years publishers will learn how to make the Internet a more powerful tool for bookselling. Right now, it's a lot of trial-and-error.

Which is all the more reason for a writer to take control.

For some writers, the idea of self-promotion is akin to peeling the living skin off their backs. They want no part of it. But writers who want to succeed in today's publishing climate, fiction or nonfiction, new media or self-published, have to engage in marketing if they hope to have any success selling their work. Even if you're lucky enough to have a publisher who will spend a few dollars on your book, you'll still bear the primary responsibility for driving sales.

Everyone believes a book tour is the be-all-and-end-all of a book launch. But increasingly, signings at bookstores are waning in popularity. Publishers are funding tours only for well-established writers, forcing new authors to either lay out their own money for a tour or to try something different. Some authors I know have recently forgone book signings for book launch parties at hip venues like art galleries, where wine and hors d'oeuvres are served, people hobnob, you get to talk for a few minutes about your new creation (or someone important interviews you), and you (it is fervently hoped) sell lots of books. At the very least, everyone has a good time.

Jane Heller is the author of thirteen chick-lit detective novels, whose latest work is a nonfiction book called *Confessions of a She-Fan: The Course of True Love With the New York Yankees*. A former publishing company marketing executive in New York, she is particularly creative when it comes to launching her books. When *Confessions of a She Fan* came out, the book launch was held at a local sports bar.

In *Some Nerve*, Heller's most recent novel, a celebrity reporter signs up as a hospital volunteer to get the story on a movie star patient. So Heller, a longtime volunteer at one of Santa Barbara's hospitals, used the hospital grounds to throw a book party.

If your publisher does allocate marketing funds for you, its publicity efforts will only last for six days to six months, after which the public relations folks will turn their attention to the next cycle of books coming out. What to do? Get savvy. Educate yourself on how to gain attention for your book.

"More than ever, publishers are unlikely to spend money or even much time on minor titles," agent Victoria Skurnick says. "And, more than ever, writers are going to have to be their own publicists. The good news is that with the Internet, this can be done."

Editor Diane Gedymin agrees:

> Authors have to fully involve themselves with new technologies and invest in their platform—virtual or otherwise. With the sophistication of the Internet world, it's not sufficient to have a cut-and-paste, static Web site, but you don't have to spend a fortune either. Again, research is essential so your site is competitive with what's out there. Publishers aren't going to do an author's work; they don't have the staff or the budget to do so.
>
> An author must be visible in every venue possible. If they're clueless about all things digital, they should take courses. You can hire someone to do backroom Internet marketing (i.e., keyword purchase) but, for the most part, no one can blog for you or engage in an online exchange of ideas. Bottom line: Learn everything you can about Internet marketing and then do everything possible to exploit every opportunity out there. Authors have to be relentless (and shameless) in promoting their books.

At the very minimum, you'll need a Web site (more on Web sites in Chapter 9) and a list of local and regional media and bookstores. Some authors hire a publicist to send out press releases,

> Publishers are funding tours only for well-established writers, forcing new authors to either lay out their own money for a tour or try something different.

set up book signings, and maybe book some speaking gigs. You should do as many press, radio, and TV interviews as you can manage.

Send a list of local media to your publisher and ask the publicity folks to send review copies to all of them. The publisher should follow up with phone calls to see if they can schedule interviews, but if the public relations folks don't, do it yourself. You should also consider blogging (but only if you can devote time to writing on a regular basis, at least every other day), and sign up for accounts on Facebook, LinkedIn, Twitter, and the leading social networking sites that fit your genre.

> "Publishers aren't going to do an author's work; they don't have the staff or the budget to do so."
>
> —editor Diane Gedymin

Novelist Christopher Moore (chrismoore.com) does all of these things and much more.

Moore, author of such zany international bestsellers as *You Suck, The Dirty Job, Lamb,* and *Fool,* is no fool when it comes to marketing his work. His relentless dedication to promotion—and his early employment of new technology like e-mail, e-newsletters, and social networks—allowed him to build a huge fan base and helped propel his books into the stratosphere on the bestseller lists.

Moore honed his writing skills at the Santa Barbara Writers Conference, where he also began to develop the networking and promotion skills he's used to great effect over the past fifteen years. When two of his books were nominated for the prestigious Quill Awards, he utilized his vast e-mail list and encouraged his fans to vote. It worked, and *The Stupidest Angel* (Science Fiction/Fantasy/Horror, 2005) and *The Dirty Job* (General Fiction, 2006) came away with top "people's choice" honors. (The Quills were suspended in 2008.)

Honestly, if Moore's books weren't laugh-out-loud funny and smart and interesting to boot, no amount of promotion would help him sell them. *Fool* is a brilliant, funny, and, yes, tragic, retelling of *King Lear,* with a little Macbeth and portions of at least ten other Shakespearean plays thrown in for good measure.

The Onion says Moore is "the thinking man's Dave Barry or the impatient man's Tom Robbins." I don't know whether that's solid or faint praise.

But his dedication to staying connected to his growing legion of fans by e-mail, e-newsletter, blog, Twitter, Facebook, and RSS (Really Simple Syndication) feeds has allowed Moore to grow his base of support and his book sales. When *Fool* debuted in early 2009, it immediately shot to No. 4 on *The New York Times* best-seller list, and long lines of fans showed up at his book signings around the country.

Moore says:

> Writers often start worrying about how to sell a book before they even have a book to sell, and while it's not a mistake to think about the commercial aspect of a novel during the concept and writing of it, that shouldn't be the dominant engine driving the project. You have to finish and you have to do your best work. We often draw a line between "published" and "nonpublished," imagining that once we sell a book we can just sit back and write like the true artists that we know we are. The truth is, whether you're an out-of-the-gate bestseller, or you build a career over years from printings of a few thousand to the bestseller list, as I did, there is no *there* there. You can always do better, you can always take on more, you are never going to master your craft (or at least I'm not), which may be the true gift of being a writer. But you have to try to improve, to understand, to reach.

Writing is only the first step, publisher Elfrieda Abbe says:

> More than ever, writers need to understand how the publishing business works and be savvy about marketing. Writers can keep up on trends and industry news by reading such publications as *Publishers Weekly* and *The Writer*. At writers conferences, they can learn the ins and outs of publishing and marketing firsthand from successful writers, editors, and publishers.

> Writers are expected to come to the table not only with a book but also with a pre-existing audience and a plan for reaching that audience or a "platform." Unless a writer is a best-selling author, it's unlikely the publisher will launch an

extensive publicity campaign for her or his book. Much of the job of getting publicity falls directly on the author's shoulders.

Writers are often expected to put on their PR hats and arrange readings, write about their work in blogs and e-newsletters, create a page on Facebook or MySpace, and upload videos on YouTube. Knowing how to use the latest technology, from cell phones to electronic readers to the latest Internet thing, to deliver content is a definite asset.

Red Room founder and author Ivory Madison says: "The biggest trend we're going to see is publishers and authors admitting that the authors have to market their books themselves and have to do it well, which means online through social networking and viral marketing tools, if they want to make a living at it. Those are two very different jobs, writing and marketing. Few people are good at both. The most successful writers will be those who take ownership of marketing their books."

Technology offers unlimited possibilities for promotion. It's just a matter of doing it. The down side, of course, is carving out the time.

Another huge unknown for writers and the publishing world today is how electronic books will affect printed matter. No one knows, but there is lots of speculation. Sales of electronic titles exploded in 2009, up 176 percent to $169.5 million, according to the Association of American Publishers. That increased the total trade share of sales for e-books in 2009 to 3.3 percent, up from 1.2 percent in 2008. Clearly there is increasing interest in the e-book format, and that trend is likely to continue, as Apple's much-heralded iPad begins to make inroads into the e-book platform market.

> Technology offers unlimited possibilities for promotion. It's just a matter of doing it. The down side, of course, is carving out the time.

So, the question for writers is, of course, will electronic books become a viable initial publishing option? Some large publishers are staggering the formats in which their new titles appear, so that a new hardback will come out in printed format, but the e-version will not be available for several months. I think this will likely go by the wayside as publishers realize they aren't forcing people to buy print books, but are losing potential sales overall.

Still, agent Jeff Herman believes it will remain a subsidiary delivery system for conventional books: "As a stand-alone, it will be one part of the overall digital universe, but far from ready to be at the vanguard on a routine basis. For self-publishers, it will be another way to beat the system and go straight to the customer, with speed and relatively little overhead."

Madison agrees: "An e-book can build a customer base for a real book. Consider the example of the software company 37Signals. They took content not directly related to their core business, blogs about the company's operations, I think, and reformatted it into an e-book which they sold to the people who had read the blog. That was so successful, with a critical mass of customers and buzz, that they turned it into a self-published book and sold it more broadly. The blog led to the e-book, which led to the book.

"I see e-books more as a marketing move and a secondary revenue stream for the content, with the book still remaining primary," Madison says. "Physical books will still be a huge industry and electronic books will only be a tiny part of that. Television didn't kill movies for a variety of reasons, and e-books will not kill the book, just as the audiobook did not kill the book."

Author Josh Conviser says: "As readers shift to e-books, the little guys will gain access to the same market that, right now, only the big boys can reach. The trick then is getting your novel to break through all the chatter and reach an audience."

What about audiobooks?

"Audios are a different world because they relate to a unique part of the mind/brain," Herman says. "E-books can be 'published' within twenty-four hours, without limit, without inventory, without much overhead, by anyone-anytime-anywhere. There might be diminished credibility because no established publisher has 'vouched' for you, which is the same challenge for self-publishing in general. But if you overcome that and penetrate your market, you will be the master of your own domain."

"The audiobook will, in my opinion, have a much wider audience and distribution than an e-book," agent Doris Booth says. "iTunes, the leading distributor of songs, for example, now accepts audiobooks from top publishers such as Audible.com (owned by Amazon). Audiobooks have greater visibility in the digital world than do e-books. Kindle will absolutely be a viable initial publishing option. The problem for the individual author is there are restrictions for being accepted into the Kindle library. You must already have a proven sales record, as I understand it. Also, be careful not to sign away all your rights to Kindle and thus thwart other digital possibilities. Amazon has become more and more proprietary in its thinking."

Publication of your book in any format makes sense—it will only add to the revenue stream and increase your exposure to an increasingly fractured reading public.

"It's time for the publicity/marketing wing of book publishing to enter a new age. Hollywood and the music industry have become masters of viral marketing. Such marketing is not expensive, but requires a new and very savvy approach to the field," Conviser says. "For bestsellers, this isn't an issue but, for the rest of us, it's unproductive to put so much of the marketing/publicity burden on the author. You'd never see a director building the Web site for his/her studio film, but that happens consistently with the major publishers. Yes, some authors are very good at selling their books, but most are better at writing them."

Unfortunately, the current state of publishing requires a writer to also become a very good marketer.

9. Web Sites and Blogging: Yes, You Should

"If you are not afraid of the voices inside you, you will not fear the critics outside you."—Natalie Goldberg

One evening at a cocktail party, you are introduced to a woman from New York. She asks what you do for a living. Most writers I know have "day jobs," so do you say, A) "I'm a probation officer for the county?" or do you say, B) "I'm a writer (poet/ screenwriter/ novelist)"? The correct answer, in case you were wondering, is B. You are a writer. Of course, the next thing she will ask is, "What have you published?"—in which case you can list your latest best-seller. Or, if you don't have one yet, you say, "I'm working on a novel about (and here you insert your thirty-second elevator pitch)."

She may be a Hollywood producer, for all you know. And, if you don't start seeing yourself as a writer, it's going to be tough to convince others that you are one. So, put on the garment and wear it around a bit. The more you try it on, the more comfortable you'll become. This is very important, because whether you are writing magazine articles, screenplays, or poems, you have to start marketing yourself and your work. Yes, yes, I know. There are plenty of famous reclusive writers like the late J.D. Salinger. You're not one of them. You can't afford not to draw attention to your work in every way possible. The key is to get maximum exposure for your book, or blog, or whatever it is you are creating.

Use your imagination. Say you've just published your first book, a memoir. The publisher is a small literary press that doesn't have a budget for promotion. How do you start? First, develop a Web site. This is critical, because almost everything else you do to promote your book will spin off of this one element. Before you look for a Web site designer, you want to secure a domain name. You should own your own name, if it's available (e.g., marciameier.com), and you should also buy a domain for the title of your book. So, for this book, I considered navigatingthepublishingworld.com, but it is too long. So I settled on navigatingpublishing.com, which works fine. And I bought the .org and .us versions, as well.

Buying a domain name is relatively inexpensive, but it can be very valuable to you over time. Initially, you want to build one Web site and have all your domain names point to it. This is an easy thing that any Webmaster can do. Eventually, you may want to have a different site for each book you write, but for now, having the domain names point to one site is sufficient.

You can also buy names that are similar to yours. For example, the Santa Barbara Writers Conference owns several variations of domain names (sbwriters.com, sbwritersconference.com, and sbwc. org). Buying several versions protects you from someone who may buy a similar name and put up a fake or competing site.

Once you have your domain names, you'll need a Web hosting service. There are a number of places to get free Web hosting. Just do a Google search for "free Web hosting," but make sure you read the fine print. A number of sites that come up under that search term actually offer services for a fee. If you're Web savvy, you can design your own site, using a simple template.

However, I recommend that you invest in having a site professionally designed. An author's Web site is usually the first place a reader will go to learn more about the book and you. Many publishers offer Web pages for their writers. That's fine.

I still think it behooves you, especially if this is your first book, to invest in a site that you have complete control over and which will serve only your interests. The best way to find a Web designer is to ask your friends who designed theirs. Or, look at the sites of other authors and contact their designers. If you work at an outside job, ask the person who maintains the company's Web site if they do design work on the side. Most do. Review at least fifteen Web sites of other authors and decide what you like and don't like about them, then present your ideas to the Web designer. If that person offers other helpful suggestions, that's great. If he or she resists your ideas, move on to the next potential designer. You want someone who will guide you with their expertise, but also honor your ideas. If you want to accomplish a certain look, the designer ought to be able to offer ideas to achieve it, particularly if yours don't quite work.

Be picky. This is your face on the World Wide Web. It is your book, your personality, your future. Ask if the designer also provides maintenance of the site once it's designed and active, and

> Invest in having a site professionally designed. An author's Web site is usually the first place a reader will go to learn more about the book and you.

how much that will cost. Many writers assume the designer will continue to update the site, but that is a separate service that you should figure into your overall monthly promotion budget. Many sites only require occasional modifications, and there are different maintenance packages you can choose. How often do you think you'd update information? Once a week? Once a month? Think about the timeliness of the content you want to put on your Web site. A calendar listing all of your book signings is a nice addition, but it also would need consistent monitoring. You might be able to achieve the same goal, which is to notify people of book signing dates, author appearances, and other news about your book, with a Twitter or Facebook account. (More on social networking in Chapter 10.)

Your Web site, or page, ought to include your bio and samples of your writing, of course. I think it's a great place to keep an archive of your writing. Include your photography, if you take pictures, and include references for editing talents or any other skills you have. Testimonials from editors or others you have worked with are always a nice touch. Add blurbs about your books or writing from other authors (which you should use in your books, as well.) Think of your Web site as your primary marketing tool. If you can't afford a personal Web site, the next best thing is an author page hosted by a site like authorsden.com or redroom.com.

> Be picky. This is your face on the World Wide Web. It is your book, your personality, your future.

Red Room, founded by Ivory Madison, is one of the best author sites I've seen. The press has called it "the Facebook for authors and readers." Madison says:

> Red Room is a community site focused on meeting every-one's needs, which in today's environment means targeting. It wouldn't do us any good to showcase the bestsellers; we need to showcase what only the one individual reader visiting our site is extremely interested in. That's targeting.
>
> We put all authors on equal footing to promote their books, and we help connect the right readers to them, and not just for the three-week window retailers are especially interested in you, but over your entire lifetime. Publisher Web sites don't successfully promote authors or sell books in any meaning-ful way. In the past couple of years, publishers have poured millions into their sites and it just doesn't work because people want a marketplace.

Blogging

One of the best ways to generate significant traffic to your Web site or author page is through blogging.

"Blogging is the most important thing to do, and a v-blog, videos, photos, press clippings, reviews, article reprints, and any other content you have should be up on your Red Room page (or whatever you use—other social networks, publisher Web sites, or a freestanding site)," Madison says. "You're having a virtual visit with someone. Let them get to know you, like you, become invested in you. When you continue to push them value, by blogging regularly, you keep the relationship going and stay top of mind, and they become invested in your writing."

What is a blog? Short for Weblog, it is essentially a daily entry into an online diary. There are news blogs, which have a serious journalistic focus. There are personal blogs, often written for family members; there are business blogs that promote a particular firm or service (your books and writing, for example); there are information blogs, i.e. on films, books, recipes, household tips, etc.; and there are political blogs, like *The Huffington Post*.

Many agents have blogs that provide information about the publishing industry. I use my blog to talk about writing generally, to promote my teaching and my own writing projects, and I will use it to market this book.

To be effective, a blog needs to be written every day, or, if that's not possible, at least every other day. In cyberspace, people expect something new every time they return to your site, so to be relevant and effective, you have to blog regularly. And you have to have something useful to say every time you blog. This is difficult, but it can be done. And a good blog can lead to other writing jobs. Rachel Thurston, a travel writer, photographer, and musician, got a lucrative magazine assignment out of blogging (rachelsthurston.com). The editor of a national women's adventure magazine happened across one of her travel blogs and invited her to write a piece for them.

In addition to being timely, the very best blogs have great writing, contain content that can't be found anywhere else, provide something no one else does (information, a service or a product), are relevant, and provide links to other sources.

One of my favorites is "The Pioneer Woman" (thepioneerwoman. com). Written by Ree Drummond, the blog is a combination of family confessional, folksy advice, stunning photography, and great recipes. Drummond is like Martha Stewart, only funnier and down-to-earth: a Martha Stewart on the range. Her blog and recipes became so popular that when she published a cookbook, *The Pioneer Woman Cooks: Recipes from an Accidental Country Girl*, in October 2009, it sold more advance copies on Amazon.com than any other title in late September. Her Web site routinely gets more than two million visitors per month.

> To be effective, a blog needs to be written every day, or, if that's not possible, at least every other day.

Growing up in Oklahoma, Drummond couldn't wait to go off to Los Angeles, where she got her degree at the University of Southern California. During a brief stay at her parents' house before she planned to move to Chicago to go to law school, she met her cowboy husband and ended up on a sprawling ranch out in the middle of nowhere. At some point, she decided to begin a blog about her ranch life, her children (four), her love affair with her "Marlboro Man," and all things domestic in Middle America. She added her recipes, with photos showing exactly how to salt that steak, for example, and household tips. Her writing is fun, funny, poignant, and sassy, which is why her blog is so interesting. Also, she blogs nearly every day, and she consistently adds new content.

"Even before you've got the publishing contract, you need readers," Ivory Madison says. "To get directly to the readers, you need to focus on leveraging your real-life network online, and locating your target readers, wherever they are, and spreading the word about yourself."

If you aren't ready to invest in a personal Web site, you can set up a free blog at BlogSpot.com. Or join one of the author sites I mentioned earlier. I occasionally blog at *The Huffington Post* (huffingtonpost.com/marcia-meier), which gives me exposure for my other work (more on how to interweave all your online sites for maximum advantage in Chapter 10), and I have blogs on both my personal Web site (marciameier.com) and my page at Red Room (redroom.com/author/marcia-meier).

"Build your audience on the Internet (or otherwise) before you approach an editor or agent," literary agent Doris Booth advises. "If you can say 25,000 or 50,000 people visit your blog every month, and they are all talking about and sharing what you're writing on the subject of, say, Yo-Yos, then you are a much more attractive candidate to become published. Build your audience as a speaker or a journalist with a huge following, in any way you can. Celebrities get published because they have vast, already-established audiences. It is harder to build an audience if you're a novelist, but not impossible. Visit the sites of successful authors such as Gayle Lynds (gaylelynds.com), Heather Graham (heathergraham.com), and James Patterson (jamespatterson.com) and see how they draw attention to their work."

The more you can leverage your intellectual property by selling your same content in a variety of formats and chunks, the better, Madison adds: "Let's take the example of a nonfiction self-help book. It used to be that you could do a seminar based on your book, create a workbook based on your book, a calendar with quotes from the book, an audiobook, maybe make a documentary or sell the movie rights. These new formats are no different."

Should you post portions of your book online for free? Amazon. com displays portions of books for sale on its site, and many experts agree it doesn't hurt. Booth says:

Generally speaking, post one chapter (fifteen to twenty pages) on the Internet. That should give an editor, agent, or reader a sense of your story and writing style. Just be sure to break the excerpt at a point where the audience will crave more.

The major publishers tell me the publication of free segments of their titles is helping rather than hindering sales. Writers may need to consider how their books will play in a world of snippets and clips. They also need to be sure that their contracts with publishers fairly compensate them if the publishers are realizing incomes from digital channels. For example, libraries will pay Google a fee for being part of its free distribution of materials in libraries. Well, if Google is being paid and the publisher is realizing income from these library fees, then the author should be compensated. These are the nuances of the industry that your agent should deal with.

Getting your book reviewed is another important marketing technique, though it is getting more difficult as newspapers and other book review sources make cutbacks. Still, a positive notice in *Publisher's Weekly*, *Kirkus Reviews*, or even, hallelujah!, *The New York Times* can increase sales of your book many times over. Reviews in local media also help to drive sales, especially if you are well-known in your community.

> "The more you can leverage your intellectual property by selling your same content in a variety of formats and chunks, the better."
> —Red Room founder Ivory Madison

If you have a traditional publisher, review copies of your book will be sent out on your behalf to your community media and the major reviewers. That's also true if you go with a quality subsidy press. With the online self-publishers, you probably will have to pay extra for that service. Or you can do it yourself.

Once you're published, as agent Paul Fedorko says: "Network, network, network." How you use your network is going to be critical to your success. Contact all the people you know in the media and book worlds and let them know about your book. Take copies to your local bookstores and ask them to arrange for a signing and to sell it on consignment. Most will be happy to accommodate you.

Go to writers conferences and introduce yourself to as many people as you can. Many conferences invite newly published authors to appear as speakers and panelists. Ask if you might be a good fit for a panel. Send out occasional missives about your latest projects to all the people on your e-mail list. Stay in regular touch with your professional contacts. Don't let a day go by that isn't devoted in some way to promoting your writing.

"YouTube, MySpace, blogs, Web sites. Go where the future goes," Ken Atchity advises. "Make a book video. Get in the news. Or become Johnny Appleseed—go out there and give your books away if you have to. Blogging is good. As traffic to your blog grows, your visibility grows. The only limits to marketing are those of your imagination, and if you don't have imagination, you aren't a writer anyway."

10. Facebook and MySpace and Tweeting, Oh My!

"The secret to being a writer is that you have to write. It's not enough to think about writing or to study literature or plan a future life as an author. You really have to lock yourself away, alone, and get to work."
—*Augusten Burroughs*

If you're not familiar with social networking sites like Facebook, MySpace, Twitter, and LinkedIn, now's the time to invest in learning about them. These networks can be tremendous tools for promoting yourself and your work, and for drawing attention to your writing.

Called a viral loop, or viral marketing, all social networking sites operate on the theory of contagion. One person reads your latest book and posts or tweets a note to all of his or her friends/followers saying, "You're got to read this!" The recipients pass it on to their friends and contacts, and pretty soon your book is on the best-seller lists. It's the Internet version of word-of-mouth advertising, and it works. When Hyperion was getting ready to launch Kelly Corrigan's memoir, *The Middle Place*, the marketing folks did a video of Corrigan reading a touching essay to the women who had supported her through her breast cancer experience, and they posted the video on Corrigan's Web page. Women passed the video to one another through viral sharing, and Corrigan's book spent twenty-seven weeks on *The New York Times* best-seller list.

If you write a column or blog, you can post a notice on Twitter, with a link to the Web site where it appears. Many writers create podcasts of their books or columns and draw attention to them with Facebook and Twitter posts. Some writers invite their followers and friends to post comments or reviews, which can then be reposted or "retweeted" for additional exposure. If I want to promote a writers event, I can send a message to all my friends on Facebook, send a mass message to everyone in my Facebook group or fan page, and tweet it with a link to the information on my Web site.

My Web site and my author page at Red Room allow me to post blogs from those spots to my Facebook page and/or other sites like MySpace and LinkedIn. And I can use Twitter to send out a tweet with a link to the blogs.

"People join social networks for a variety of reasons: to socialize, share, and/or self-promote," Penny Sansevieri writes in her book, *Red Hot Internet Publicity: An Insider's Guide to Marketing Your Book on the Internet.* "The one caveat to this is that social networks are not receptive to marketing messages or sales hype, but those sitting on these sites are looking for answers and advice. In fact, your presence on a social networking site should be 80 percent education and 20 percent sales. Users on social networking sites want friends, mentors, experts, and guidance."

For the uninitiated, Facebook and MySpace—and especially Twitter—can seem like alien cultures. What are they? How do they work? Why should a writer get involved?

The key is to discover how to make what is primarily an information exchange work for you. The most successful use of social media is to offer something of value. Maybe it is tips on writing through your blog, or information on your upcoming book signings, or perhaps it is "retweeting" interesting tweets from others, so that those who follow you can also get the information.

First, though, decide what your ultimate goal is. Do you want to sell your books? Connect with potential readers? Advertise appearances? Create a fan base? All of the above? Once you know what you want to accomplish, you can devise a plan to get the best and highest use out of social media.

MySpace, which was the first social network to become popular, continues to be used mostly by teenagers and young adults. Many writers, particularly younger ones, maintain a presence on MySpace.

LinkedIn is geared toward professional and business people. You can post a job opening or a resume, find customers for your products, or simply let everyone know what you're doing at any given moment. More and more people are joining LinkedIn and other social networks that target a specific audience.

Facebook, though, which was created by a student at Harvard in 2004, has become the fastest-growing social network (four hundred million and counting) and the median age of users is now 35–64. Essentially, it's an office watercooler, where everyone gathers to gab, swap gossip, and share information. Like the others, a Facebook account is free, and once you learn the ins and outs of gathering friends, posting notices to your wall or someone else's, and using the interior e-mail system, it's fairly simple.

Make sure you personalize your Facebook site with a photo and fill out as much of the bio information as possible. That information will serve to connect you to like-minded folks and allow others to find you.

Besides a Facebook personal page, you may want to create either a Facebook "group" or, probably more appropriate, a "fan page" for your books, speaking engagements, or other related events.

A "group" provides for more personal interaction and is set up and connected to a specific user. "Pages" are more appropriate for businesses, celebrities, musical groups, etc. Both allow for direct e-mail messages to be sent to the members of the group or the fans of the page, but in the case of groups, the message comes from you, the creator of the group, whereas with pages, the message comes from the entity the page is set up for. Also, groups can be selective, meaning the administrator can limit who is allowed to join, while anyone can become a fan of a page.

"Groups are great for organizing on a personal level and for smaller scale interaction around a cause," advises Mashable.com, a guide to social media. "Pages are better for brands, businesses, bands, movies, or celebrities who want to interact with their fans or customers without having them connected to a personal account, and have a need to exceed Facebook's 5,000-friend cap."

> Essentially, Facebook is an office watercooler, where everyone gathers to gab, swap gossip, and share information.

As always, the key is to refrain from the hardsell and to provide information and news that is usable and valuable to group members or fans.

Twitter, of course, is all the rage. Do you know how to tweet? A tweet is simply a post on Twitter, a declaration of no more than one hundred and forty characters. Some tweets are banal descriptions of what someone happens to be doing right then. But more than ever, those who tweet are using the system for sharing urgent or important information, for updating friends or fans on upcoming publications or events, or to find out the latest news from around the world. When a plane landed in the Hudson River in early 2009, the first news and photos from the scene were posted on Twitter. During the uprising of the Iranian elections later that year, Twitter became an important source of information, bringing the latest news of protests to the entire world.

The most effective use of your tweets not only engages your "followers," but also builds your credibility. When you tweet, consider: Is the information useful in some way to others? Does it contribute to understanding more about you, your books, and/or the writing industry? Does it provide additional information or links to other sources? Retweeting a post can be an effective way to build value.

While there are varying opinions on this, I think it's also advisable to be judicious in how often you tweet. Especially if you have Twitter linked to other social media, you don't want to annoy people with a steady bombardment. Tweeting several times a day with useful information, a repost of writing industry news, or a pithy observation about writing is probably enough.

Other tools to incorporate into your Web site and marketing efforts include RSS feeds, podcasts, and V-logs.

An RSS (Really Simple Syndication) feed is a tool that allows you to push information out to readers. Essentially, it allows you to syndicate your blog, or whatever the latest news is from your Web site. Readers subscribe by clicking on the RSS symbol on your site, which initiates a subscription process. Then anytime you post new information, it automatically sends an e-mail or downloads it to an RSS feed reader on the subscriber's Web site. If you have a personalized Web page service like iGoogle or MyYahoo, RSS feeds are used to place the content you requested (news, weather, stock quotes) on your site. You can use the same technology to feed your followers or friends updates from your Web site.

> First, decide what your ultimate goal is. Do you want to sell your books? Connect with potential readers? Advertise appearances? Create a fan base? All of the above?

Podcasts are simple to create and easy to post on iTunes or on your own Web site. A podcast is an audio file that can be downloaded to any Web site or MP3 player. Ernie Witham, the author and columnist I wrote about in Chapter 5, creates a podcast based on his column every week, posts it on his Web site and iTunes, and also sends it via RSS to those who subscribe.

Just as blog is short for Web log, V-log is short for video log. V-logs can be used to promote a new book, to send out a visual newsletter or blog, or to create an infomercial for your Web site. If you're a nonfiction author with a how-to book, you can use V-logs to explain how to use a product or service.

Catherine Ryan Hyde, author of thirteen novels, seven of which are for young adults, has created V-log trailers for several of her novels, and she has created podcasts, too, all of which you can find on her Web site, catherineryanhyde.com. She also has V-logs of her reading excerpts from her books, which is a very effective way to introduce someone to your work.

Remember to be creative and have fun. The most popular videos on YouTube are humorous. Tweets from Christopher Moore (twitter.com/authorguy), the author I wrote about in Chapter 8, are just as funny as his books.

"A friend recently asked me about the strategy behind my constant Facebook profile photo changes and status updates," Jeff Van-

---

Creating a Simple V-Log

1. Write a short script (essay, book trailer, product instructions, etc.) that can be read in less than ten minutes.

2. Digitally videotape yourself reading the script (about 0.5 gigabyte of memory). Use a mirror behind the camera to ensure that you are in the shot.

3. Convert the format of the recording from AVI to Mpeg (software to do this is available online at www.avi-mpeg-converter.net).

4. Open a free account at YouTube.com.

5. Upload the V-log to YouTube, where you'll receive a code that you can then use to place the V-log on your Web site.

6. Share the V-log by sending the code to friends.

(Thanks to my friend Sally Franz, humorist and producer of babyboomertalkradio.com and author of the forthcoming memoir *Scrambled Leggs: A Snarky Tale of Hospital Hooey*, for these directions.)

---

derMeer wrote in an essay for *Publishers Weekly*. "This gave me a bit of a chuckle, because the fact is, my Facebook 'strategy' is simply to have fun. But my friend's question speaks to something we as writers seem to have lost sight of in our quest to gain leverage through the Wild West of new media platforms: Having fun and expressing creativity are sometimes the best ways to advance your career."

> V-logs can be used to promote a new book, to send out a visual newsletter or blog, or to create an infomercial for your Web site.

VanderMeer, author of *Booklife: Strategies & Survival Tips for the 21st-Century Writer*, says that just being himself on Facebook has also inadvertently led to more writing opportunities. In one case, a noted West Coast graphic artist contacted him through Facebook, which resulted in collaboration on an anthology. In another, an interview with the Texas-based owner of a giant rodent called a capybara resulted in tens of thousands of new readers of his blog.

"About four thousand of them stuck around to explore my Web site. Some of them have returned to read more. Some of them will buy my books....Was it part of a larger strategy? Did it fit into my personal mission statement, or my short-term or long-term goals? No, I did it because I thought it would be fun," VanderMeer explains.

So, learn how to use these social network tools and have fun in the process. The payoff could be your bestseller.

11. Don't Give Up

"You must keep sending work out; you must never let a manuscript do nothing but eat its head off in a drawer. You send that work out again and again, while you're working on another one. If you have talent, you will receive some measure of success—but only if you persist."—Isaac Asimov

Writing can be a discouraging business. Rejection comes from every direction. Freelance pitches are declined, poetry and short story submissions are ignored or greeted with "try again another time," and book proposals land on desks and sit for six months unanswered. It can be downright depressing. And it doesn't help that most writers toil alone. Whether you're writing full-time or eking out writing time after a full day of working for someone else, the biggest challenge is to keep writing when it seems you're Sisyphus, pushing a rock uphill.

And yet, there's that one rejection letter that offers a teeny bit of encouragement, that first poem that finds a home in an obscure literary magazine, that one agent who asks to see more of your work. Those are what we cling to, and savor. Those small forward movements—and faith in our writing—are what keep us going.

Because writing is such a singularly solitary experience, writers also need to connect with other writers, to compare work, to discuss writing and its ups and downs, and to keep focused on that next freelance assignment or short story acceptance.

Writers conferences are great for this, and I recommend you attend at least one every year or two. Consider it part of your job as a writer. More than half of the writers who attended the Santa Barbara conference in any given year had attended in the past, and many came every year. The best writers conferences offer workshops where you can receive feedback on your work-in-progress. Many conferences consist of two or three days of speakers who talk at you about writing, and that's fine. But if you really want to learn something, you have to go to one—like the Santa Barbara conference—that focuses on craft through reading and critiquing.

Also, connect with a small group of other writers to meet regularly and critique your work. I'm often asked how to join a writers group. The best answer is, start your own. Most successful writers groups come about naturally when a handful of writers become friends and decide to meet. And the most successful meet on a routine basis and have structured critique times.

I belong to a group of writers who go to a small seaside town for a week every six months to write. It's easily the most productive time for me as a writer. We don't typically read our work to the group—many of us already belong to a read-and-critique group—but we go because it allows us unfettered time to write. It provides time away from families and distractions at home, like jobs, laundry, washing dishes, cleaning the house, and caring for children and animals. It's heaven, frankly. We write all day, breaking for lunch together, and end the day with dinner and drinks, camaraderie, and lots of laughter.

One of my friends from this group has found increasing success with her diligence and commitment to her writing. Melinda Palacio was a newspaper feature writer for a number of years before she came to the Santa Barbara Writers Conference in 2001 and began writing fiction and poetry.

"A lot of what I learned has come out of the conference," Palacio says.

Palacio is both deliberate and strategic in how she sends out her work. She researches the various literary magazines, print and online, gauging which would be most likely to publish her poems and short stories. She submits several stories or poems every month, making sure she follows all the guidelines of each publication.

> Most successful writers groups come about naturally when a handful of writers become friends and decide to meet. And the most successful meet on a routine basis and have structured critique times.

Her first published short story appeared in an anthology called *Latinos in Lotusland: An Anthology of Contemporary Southern California Literature.*

"I had a hunch that this anthology was going to be very important and I was determined to see my name listed as a California author," Palacio says. "The Internet grapevine picked up editor Daniel Olivas's call in 2005 for submissions by Chicano and Latino writers. He was overwhelmed by the response. I sent three stories from my growing collection, *Bathroom Girls: Growing up in South Central Los Angeles*. And he didn't really take to them. So I sent him a story, 'The Last Time,' that won an award at SBWC in 2005, and he said he loved it."

Latinos in Lotusland was published in April 2008 by Arizona State University's Bilingual Press.

"So many wonderful things have come out of that anthology," Palacio says. "The story was a gift, one of those, what I call, quick-lightning writings. I must have written the story in fifteen minutes. Sometimes I read a book, like Marilynne Robinson's *Gilead*, that opens my eyes to new possibilities in fiction. Writing from the perspective of a father talking to his daughter was a new idea for me. The piece was so much fun to write and it happened to be under one thousand words. I remember changing the ending of the story to match the conference's contest theme, 'The Last Time.'"

She continued to send out her poems and short stories.

"I was hesitant to send out my novel because I knew it needed work. One thing I was consistent in was sending out my short stories and poetry for publication. I've received hundreds of rejections. In 2006, I started receiving acceptance letters, and some cash, from editors."

A year later, in 2007, Palacio won the PEN Center USA Emerging Voices Rosenthal Fellowship, an eight-month program for writers in the early stages of their careers. Palacio says:

"This program helped me see myself as a writer. Confidence can go a long way. The confidence-building by the faculty at the Santa Barbara Writers Conference, by my mentors at PEN, by Denise Chávez and Daniel Olivas, by my friends and fellow writers, fueled my momentum. After completing the PEN fellowship, I was eager for literary doors to open for me."

> "One thing I was consistent in was sending out my short stories and poetry for publication. I've received hundreds of rejections. In 2006, I started receiving acceptance letters, and some cash, from editors."
>
> —author Melinda Palacio

She finished her novel in late 2007 and started approaching agents, editors, and publishers. Palacio remarks:

"I sent my novel to sixteen agents, eight contests, and four publishers. Some of the agents never got back to me. I was having better luck gaining direct access to publishers through the recommendations of already established friends, such as Reyna Grande, author of *Across a Hundred Mountains* and *Dancing with Butterflies*."

In early 2009, she decided to send the novel to the same people who published *Latinos in Lotusland*. Several months later, Bilingual

Press publisher Gary Keller asked to see the full manuscript of *Ocotillo Dreams* and, three weeks later, he accepted it for publication.

Also that summer, she received a scholarship to attend the Community of Writers for a week of poetry at Squaw Valley, California:

"A month later, I received a phone call from Arthur Dawson at Kulupi Press, telling me I had won their Sense of Place Poetry Chapbook Contest. I now have a poetry chapbook, *Folsom Lockdown*, and a forthcoming novel, *Ocotillo Dreams*."

It's a wonderful story, one that continues to evolve. It's worth noting, too, that Palacio has done all of this without an agent.

One of the most inspiring stories I know that illustrates the importance of persistence is that of Selden Edwards. For more than thirty years, Edwards worked consistently on a novel, crafting, revising, and rewriting. It was truly a labor of love. Finally, after receiving rejection after rejection, in 2007, Edwards sent it to a content editor in New York who had been recommended to him. Patrick LoBrutto, a former editor with a number of New York publishers, including Ace Books, Doubleday, M. Evans, Kensington, Stealth Press (an Internet publisher), and Bantam, worked with Edwards on the book for several months. Finally, satisfied that it was ready, LoBrutto told Scott Miller, an agent with Trident Media Group in New York, about the book and suggested Edwards send it to him. Nine days after Edwards sent off the manuscript, Miller called and offered to represent him. Two weeks later, Dutton's Penguin imprint bought the novel for $750,000.

Edwards' *The Little Book* was published in fall 2008. It's a tale of time travel and improbable encounters between a 1980s rock star, Wheeler Burden, and famous people from 1897 Vienna, including Sigmund Freud and Gustav Mahler.

Publisher's Weekly said of the book: "Edwards has great fun with time travel paradoxes and anachronisms, but the real romance in this book is with the period, topped by nostalgia for the old-school American elite, as represented by the we-all-went-to-the-same-prep-school Burdens. This novel ends up a sweet, wistful elegy to the fantastic promise and failed hopes of the 20th century."

Before long, *The Little Book* was listed on a number of national best-seller lists, including the Indy List top 10 and *The New York Times* list. It also was chosen for a number of "Best of 2008" lists. When the paperback came out, it was chosen as Costco's book-of-the-month in the company's newsletter, which goes to eight million people.

Edwards has been walking on clouds ever since, and he sold a second novel to Dutton on the strength of *The Little Book's* sales. This is a story of hard work, yes, but also of perseverance. Edwards toiled for a long time, rewriting and revising. Ultimately, it paid off.

"Writers shouldn't worry about the 'industry,'" Ivory Madison cautions. "They should focus on following their dream, the creative and life-changing part of the dream. Books transform individuals and societies, and the business of books should not be mistaken for the magic and humanity of books, which is why we got in the business in the first place."

Whenever someone asks me for advice, I always say: Put your bottom in a chair and write every day. Persevere. Don't let rejection—even over a long period of time—dissuade you from your dreams. Keep writing and keep learning. Listen to constructive criticism and take it to heart if it resonates with you—and especially if more than one person tells you the same thing.

And, always, believe in yourself and your work.

Index of Contributors

Elfrieda Abbe, publisher, *The Writer* magazine

Elfrieda Abbe is publisher of *The Writer* magazine, which received the Folio Award for editorial excellence. She has been a freelance writer, staff writer, and editor at newspapers and magazines. She was previously editor of the award-winning arts and entertainment section of *The Milwaukee Sentinel* and editor of publications at the University of Wisconsin-Milwaukee College of Arts and Science.

Elfrieda Abbe, publisher
The Writer Magazine
P.O. Box 1612
Waukesha, WI 53187-1612
eabbe@kalmbach.com
Kalmbach.com

Laurie Abkemeier, literary agent, DeFiore and Company, New Jersey

A successful editor who became an agent in 2003, Laurie represents nonfiction exclusively. She has placed more than forty books with Algonquin, Atria, Ballantine, Broadway, Citadel Press/Kensington, William Morrow, HarperCollins, Three Rivers/Crown, Perigee, Penguin, Berkley, NAL, Touchstone/Fireside, Rodale, Running Press, Sasquatch, St. Martin's Press,

Ten Speed, Wiley, and Warner/Grand Central (Hachette). Laurie represents John Grogan, author of the megaseller *Marley & Me*.

Laurie Abkemeier, Literary Agent
DeFiore and Company, New Jersey
lma@defioreandco.com
defioreandco.com

Ken Atchity, COO and chairman, Atchity Entertainment International, Inc., Los Angeles

With more than forty years experience in the publishing world, and over fifteen years in entertainment, Dr. Ken Atchity is a self-defined "story merchant"—writer, producer, teacher, and literary manager, responsible for launching dozens of books and films. His life's passion is finding great storytellers and turning them into best-selling authors and screenwriters. Ken has produced twenty-eight films and written fourteen books. Based on his own teaching and writing experience, Ken has successfully built best-selling careers for novelists, nonfiction writers, and screenwriters from the ground up. Ken's Story Merchant companies (aeionline.com and thewriterslifeline.com) provide a one-stop, full-service development and management machine for commercial and literary writers who wish to launch their storytelling in all media —from publishing and film and television production to Web presence and merchandising and licensing.

Ken Atchity, Chairman
Atchity Entertainment International, Inc. (AEI)
kja@aeionline.com
thewriterslifeline.com
aeionline.com
kenatchity.blogspot.com

Doris Booth, manager, Authorlink Literary Group, Irving, Texas

Doris Booth is the manager of Authorlink Literary Group, which operates as a separate division of Authorlink.com. The agency represents true crime, thrillers, women's fiction, and a wide range of nonfiction. Recent sales have included projects for Berkley/Penguin Group USA, St. Martin's Press, and Barnes & Noble Publishing. Booth represents *New York Times* best-selling authors Stephen G. Michaud and Hugh Aynesworth, among others. In her role as the CEO of Authorlink.com, she has facilitated the sale of more than 90 fiction and nonfiction properties within the past five years, including a recent six-figure deal to HarperCollins. She has overseen direct sales to Simon & Schuster, John Wiley & Sons, McGraw-Hill, Barnes & Noble Publishing, and others. Authorlink.com is the news, information, and marketing site for editors, agents, and writers, and attracts nearly one million visitors per year.

> Doris Booth, Editor-in-Chief, Authorlink.com
> Manager, Authorlink Literary Group
> dbooth@authorlink.com
> authorlink.com
> authorlink.blogspot.com

David Cole, publisher, Bay Tree Publishing, Point Richmond, CA

David Cole has spent almost thirty years in book publishing, with stints in editing, production, publicity, marketing, and management. His company, Bay Tree Publishing, focuses on nonfiction works in the areas of business, personal finance, psychology, health, memoirs, and current affairs. The company's Ardenwood imprint provides publishing services and copublishing to authors. David is the author of three nonfiction books, including *The Complete Guide to Book Marketing*. The founder and first president of the San Francisco Bay Area Book Festival, he also served as an instructor in the University of California Extension certificate program in publishing. He has served on the board of directors of the Independent Book Publishers Association (formerly PMA) and is a board member of the Northern California Book Publicity and Marketing Association (NCBPMA).

David Cole, Publisher
Bay Tree Publishing
P.O. Box 70236
Pt. Richmond, CA 94807
dcole@baytreepublish.com
baytreepublish.com

Josh Conviser, screenwriter and novelist

Josh Conviser is a screenwriter and author of the techno-thrillers *Echelon* (2006) and *Empyre* (2008). He was the executive consultant on HBO's hit series *Rome*, and has several films in development.

Josh Conviser, Author
joshconviser@gmail.com
joshconviser.com

N. Frank Daniels, author

myspace.com/nfrankdaniels
harpercollins.com/authors/34257/N_Frank_Daniels

David Ebershoff, editor-at-large, The Random House Publishing Group, New York

David Ebershoff is the author of three best-selling novels—*The 19th Wife*, *Pasadena*, and *The Danish Girl*—and a short-story collection, *The Rose City*. His fiction has won a number of awards and has been translated into fifteen languages to critical acclaim. He teaches in the graduate writing program at Columbia University and is an editor-at-large at Random House in New York City.

David Ebershoff, Editor-at-Large
The Random House Publishing Group
1745 Broadway
New York, NY 10019
debershoff@randomhouse.com
randomhouse.com

Paul Fedorko, literary agent, N.S. Bienstock, Inc., New York

Having built his career on the publishing side of the business—at Dell/ Delacorte, Bantam, Simon and Schuster, and William Morrow—Paul Fedorko brings his wide array of publishing experience and unique skills, plus a diverse list of clients, to N.S. Bienstock of New York. Following the worldwide success of John Perkins' *Confessions of an Economic Hit Man* (both in hardcover and trade paperback), his latest success, *The Secret History of the American Empire*, leads a list of recently published books, including Jack Cafferty's *It's Getting Ugly Out There*, George Shuman's *Last Breath* (and his latest Sherry Moore novel, *Lost Girls*), Kimberly Dozier's *Breathing the Fire*, Richard Engel's *War Journal*, Gary Perkinson and T. J. Tomasi's *When Bad Things Happen to Bad Golfers*, Kathy Haines' new Rosie Winter WWII novel, *The Winter of Her Discontent*, Jane and Michael Hoffman's *Green*, and Ron McLarty's newest novel, *Art in America*.

Paul Fedorko, Literary Agent
N.S. Bienstock, Inc.
250 west 57th Street
Suite 333
New York, NY 10107
pfedorko@nsbtalent.com

Diane Gedymin, book consultant & co-author of *Get Published! Professionally, Affordably, Fast*

Diane Gedymin, an experienced veteran of the book publishing industry, provides professional consulting to authors, agents, and book publishers. She was most recently the executive editorial director of Author Solutions, which includes the self-publishing service providers iUniverse, AuthorHouse, and Xlibris; she was vice president and editorial director of iUniverse prior to the merger. With over thirty years of experience in traditional publishing at top companies, Diane has worked in nearly every area of the business, including as a literary agent affiliated with Carlisle & Company (now Inkwell); senior vice president and publisher of Harper-SanFrancisco, where she acquired and edited Sidney Poitier's #1 *New York Times* best-selling autobiography, *The Measure of a Man* (an Oprah book club selection); and as vice president and senior editor at the Putnam/Berkley Group, where she acquired Sheri Reynolds, whose novel *The Rapture of Canaan* was Oprah's third book club selection and also a #1 *New York Times* bestseller. She is the co-author of *Get Published! Professionally, Affordably, Fast*, an Amazon.com and BN.com bestseller.

Diane Gedymin
dianegedymin1@aol.com

John Grogan, author

johngrogan.com

Jeff Herman, principal, Jeff Herman Literary Agency, and author, *Jeff Herman's Guide to Book Publishers, Editors and Literary Agents*

Jeff Herman founded The Jeff Herman Literary Agency, LLC in 1987, while still in his twenties. The agency has sold hundreds of titles to publishers, and is one of the most dynamic and innovative agencies in the business. Herman's agency has a strong presence in general adult nonfiction, including business, general reference, commercial self-help, technology, recovery/healing, and spiritual subjects. Herman's own publications include *Jeff Herman's Guide to Book Publishers, Editors and Literary Agents* (more than 350,000 copies sold) and *Write the Perfect Book Proposal: 10 Proposals That Sold and Why*. His books are considered to be among the best tools available to writers. He's also the cofounder of his own indie house, Three Dog Press (3dp). Previously, Herman worked for a New York public relations firm, where he designed and managed national consumer marketing campaigns for Nabisco Brands and AT&T. Prior to that he was a publicist at Schocken Books, now a Random House imprint, where he promoted the bestseller *When Bad Things Happen to Good People*.

Jeff Herman, Literary Agent and Author
The Jeff Herman Agency
PO Box 1522
Stockbridge, MA 01262
submissions@jeffherman.com
jeffherman.com

Ivory Madison, author and founder, RedRoom.com

Red Room (redroom.com) founder and CEO Ivory Madison is a writer, editor, and entrepreneur whose goal is to create a supportive online ecosystem for the entire publishing industry from creator to consumer, because "books transform individuals and whole societies." A former management consultant to start-ups and the Fortune 500, Madison combines her business acumen with her love of writing. Before launching redroom.com, which the press has called "the Facebook for authors and readers," she founded the Red Room Writers Society in 2002, where she personally helped hundreds of aspiring and professional writers complete their books. As a result, Madison was named "Best Writing Coach" by *San Francisco* magazine. Trained as an attorney, Madison's legal career highlights included being editor-in-chief of her school's Law Review, interning at the California Supreme Court, and serving as a Law Fellow for Americans United for Separation of Church and State. Her adventures also include episodes as a New Orleans restaurateur and radical feminist politico. Her noir graphic novel, *Huntress: Year One*, was published by DC Comics in 2009; it tells the origin story of a strong female superhero.

Ivory S. Madison, J.D. CEO, Red Room Omnimedia Corporation
ivorymadison@redroom.com
redroom.com

Bob Mayer, bestselling author and speaker

Bob Mayer is the *New York Times* best-selling author of more than forty books, both fiction and nonfiction. His books have hit the *New York Times*, *Wall Street Journal*, *Publishers Weekly*, *USA Today* and other best-seller lists. He has more than three million books in print. He's the author of *The Novel Writers Toolkit: A Guide to Writing Great Fiction and Getting It Published* and *Who Dares Wins: The Green Beret Way to Conquer Fear & Succeed*.

Bob Mayer
PO Box 392
Langley, WA 98260
bob@bobmayer.org
bobmayer.org

Ron McLarty, author

ronmclarty.com

Christopher Moore, author

chrismoore.com

Bonnie Nadell, principal, Frederick Hill Bonnie Nadell Agency, Los Angeles

Bonnie Nadell is president of the Frederick Hill Bonnie Nadell literary agency in Los Angeles. She represents writers of both fiction and nonfiction, including Nicole Mones, Sonia Nazario, Antonya Nelson, Davida Wills Hurwin, Rebecca Solnit, and the late David Foster Wallace.

Bonnie Nadell, Literary Agent
Fred Hill Bonnie Nadell Agency
8899 Beverly Blvd., Suite 805
Los Angeles, CA 90048
fredhillbnadell@sbcglobal.net

Dan Poynter, author and founder, ParaPublishing, Santa Barbara, California

Dan Poynter is the author of more than 125 books, including his international bestseller, *The Self-Publishing Manual: How to Write, Print and Sell Your Own Book*, as well as *Writing Nonfiction*, *The Skydiver's Handbook*, and *The Expert Witness Handbook*. His seminars have been featured on CNN, his books have been reviewed in the *Wall Street Journal*, and his story has been told in *U.S. News & World Report*. The second volume of *The Self-Publishing Manual*, featuring new information on using social media like Facebook and Twitter, was published in early 2009.

Dan Poynter, Author and Founder
Para Publishing
P.O. Box 8206
Santa Barbara, CA 93118-8206
DanPoynter@ParaPublishing.com
ParaPublishing.com

Morris Rosenthal, author and owner, Foner Books

Morris Rosenthal is a trade author and self-publisher whose works include the groundbreaking *Print-on-Demand Book Publishing* (2004), which first introduced authors and publishers to the Internet-centric business model paired with short-discount POD distribution. Rosenthal has been publishing online since 1995, and since 2005 he has authored the top self-publishing blog at fonerbooks.com/cornered.htm. Long known in online publishing circles for his early work in reverse-engineering the Amazon sales rank system, he's also an outspoken advocate of e-books and intellectual property rights. A series of short video lectures on publishing topics originally published for his Self Publishing 2.0 blog are available at YouTube.com/fonerbooks.

Morris Rosenthal, Author and Owner
Foner Books
morris@fonerbooks.com
fonerbooks.com

Victoria Skurnick, literary agent, Levine Greenberg Literary Agency, New York

Victoria Skurnick joined the Levine Greenberg Literary Agency in 2007. Before that, she was editor-in-chief of The Book-of-the-Month Club. Her other jobs in trade publishing include both editorial and marketing stints at Holt, Rinehart and Winston, Avon Books, Pocket Books, and St. Martin's Press. Since she became an agent, she has sold books as diverse as *The Dangerous Book for Dogs* to Random House, *Old City Hall*, a legal thriller, to Farrar, Straus & Giroux, and *Critical*, a look at health care by former Senator Tom Daschle.

Victoria Skurnick, Literary Agent
Levine Greenberg Literary Agency
307 Seventh Avenue, Suite 2407
New York, NY 10001
vskurnick@levinegreenberg.com
levinegreenberg.com

Michelle Theall, founder, *Women's Adventure* magazine

Michelle Theall started *Women's Adventure* magazine in 2003 as the only women's specific adventure sports and travel title on newsstands worldwide. The magazine quickly won accolades, garnering the prestigious Folio Award for editorial excellence and was named one of the top thirty best launches by *Mr. Magazine*. In 2008, Theall sold the title to Big Earth Publishing, owners of several book houses, including Bleak House mysteries, Trails Books, Westcliffe Publishers, Intrigue Press, and others. Theall continues to run the magazine division for Big Earth publishing and will consider magazine queries and book proposals for *Women's Adventure* and other book publishing houses included under the Big Earth umbrella. Theall began her career in publishing in the 1990s with *Women's Sports + Fitness* magazine, where she helped launch the first-ever high school and college women's sports magazines. When the titles sold to and were absorbed by *CondeNast*, Theall did consulting work for niche magazines, including *VeloNews, Inside Triathlon, Freeskier, Blue, Elevation,* and *Alternative Medicine*. In 2006, she landed a multibook contract with Fulcrum Publishing and a syndicated column on health and fitness with McClatchy-Tribune. Her *Little Kick in the Butt* book series remains one of Fulcrum Publishing's best-selling titles. Theall has appeared on NBC, The Travel Channel, "The Montel Williams Show," and the Fox Sports Network as part of her writer/author platform in health and fitness.

Michelle Theall
VP Magazine Division / Big Earth
Editor-in-chief / Creative Director of Women's Adventure
1637 Pearl St., Suite 201
Boulder, CO 80302
bigearthpublishing.com
womensadventuremagazine.com
magazineconference.com

Michael Todd, online editor, *Miller-McCune* magazine

Michael Todd is the online editor of the Miller-McCune Center for Research, Media, and Public Policy, which sponsors the research-based, solutions-oriented news Web site Miller-McCune.com. Although just prior to joining the center he was managing editor of the national magazine *Hispanic Business*, most of his twenty-five-year career had been spent in newspaper journalism, ranging from papers in the Marshall Islands to tiny California farming communities. The decision to enter journalism was made almost on a lark, as having discovered in college that a planned career as a physicist was going to be really hard, he opted to enter newspapering as a chance to both write and get paid for it. He was half-right, and the blunder taught him the importance of doing his homework before taking on any future assignment.

Michael Todd, Editor
Miller-McCune Magazine Online
michael.todd@miller-mccune.com
miller-mccune.com

Glossary of Selected Terms

Advance—An amount of money given to an author upon signing a contract to write a book. Advances are funds advanced against expected future royalty payments to the author. The publisher is betting that your book will make at least enough money for themselves to generate royalties to you, the author, equal to the advance. If the book pulls in revenue beyond that, you earn additional royalties as a percentage of total sales once the advance is paid back to the publisher (see below). If it makes less, you still get to keep the advance, which will come in handy because the publisher probably won't buy another book from you.

Agent—If you write fiction, you need one. A good agent represents all your interests in the book world, from negotiating your book contracts, to suggesting changes to your novel or nonfiction book, to assuring you for the umpteenth time that, yes, you are a good writer.

Audiobook—A novel or nonfiction book that has been put on audio CD.

Big House Publisher—One of the top publishing houses in the country, all based in New York. These include Houghton Mifflin Harcourt, Harlequin, Simon and Schuster, Hyperion, Penguin, Farrar, Straus, and Giroux, HarperCollins, Rodale, Scholastic, St. Martins Press, Random House, Henry Holt and Company, Kensington, W.W. Norton, John Wiley and Sons, and Time Warner.

Blog—What every writer should be doing to develop a platform and market his or her work. If it can be done on the writer's own Web site, that's ideal. It involves writing a short essay frequently—every day if possible.

Copyright—Copyright is complicated, but essentially everything you write is your intellectual property and is protected by law. You have the right to give away or sell certain aspects of your property—including audio, electronic, movie, and foreign rights—which is what you do when you sign a book contract. Your agent (see above) is supposed to protect all those rights and, should you desire to sell them, get as much money as possible for them.

E-book— Electronic book. The latest thing in the publishing world, e-books are downloaded to an electronic reader about the size of a trade paperback. Amazon's Kindle so far has dominated the market. Barnes & Noble has one called the Nook, and SONY's version is called the Reader. Apple has a brand-new e-book called the iPad, which offers an entirely new platform. It's expected to offer a serious challenge to Kindle.

Editor—A publishing house editor is actually more engaged in the acquisition of new books than in the process of editing. Many writers today must hire an independent line-and-content editor to get their book in shape before sending it to an agent.

E-zine—Another new term from the world of the Internet. An e-zine is an online magazine where many former journalists are hoping to find jobs.

Hardcover—The Holy Grail of books. Hardcovers are perceived as the highest-quality level of publishing a book, especially for a novelist.

New Media—Any of a number of online opportunities and tools for writers, including e-zines, blogging, Twittering, and using social network sites like Facebook and MySpace for marketing.

POD—Print-on-demand, the process of printing a book electronically. It allows for the instant printing of a book, one copy at a time, at nearly the same quality as a book printed by a publisher on an offset press.

Publishing Contract—Every writer's dream. A contract specifies the rights and obligations of both the publishing house and the writer, and its negotiation is usually best handled by an agent or literary attorney who understands the nuance of literary contract law.

Returns (or Remainders)—The worst possible fate for your book. It means the bookstores were unable to sell the books they ordered, and so they get to return them to the publisher for full credit. This is an awful practice that makes it virtually impossible to know how many books you've actually sold and seriously affects your bottom line.

Royalties—Oh, Happy Day! If you are earning royalties, it means your book has sold enough to pay back your advance to the publisher and now you're getting a percentage of the purchase price of the books sold.

Self-publishing—Used to be the kiss of death for a writer. Some people believe it still is, but self-publishing is becoming more and more respectable by the day. Some authors have used self-publication to ultimately sell their books to publishing houses.

Twitter—Social network whereby one tells the entire world (or at least those people who have asked to "follow" you online) what you are doing at any given moment. "Tweets" can be no more than 140 words at a time. Savvy people are starting to use Twitter, Facebook, and MySpace to effectively promote and market their writing.

Vanity, or Subsidy, Press—A publishing company that offers assistance in editing, production, printing, and distribution of your book, services which you pay for.

V-log—An online video promoting your book.

Resources for Writers

BOOKS ON THE CRAFT OF WRITING

Artists & Writers Colonies, by Gail Hellund Bowler (Blue Heron Publishing)

Bird by Bird: Some Instructions on Writing and Life, by Anne Lamott (Anchor Books)

Creative Nonfiction, by Philip Gerard (Story Press)

From Where You Dream, by Robert Olen Butler (Grove Press)

Making a Literary Life, by Carolyn See (Ballantine Books)

On Becoming a Novelist, by John Gardner (W.W. Norton & Co.)

On Writing: A Memoir of the Craft, by Stephen King (Pocket Books)

On Writing Well, by William Zinsser (HarperPerennial)

The Art of Time in Memoir, Sven Birkerts (Graywolf Press)

The Elements of Style, by Strunk and White (Macmillan Publishing)

The Novel Writer's Toolkit: How to Write Your Novel and Get it Published, by Bob Mayer (Writers Digest Books)

The Poetry Home Repair Manual, by Ted Kooser (University of Nebraska Press)

Writing Fiction: The Practical Guide from New York's Acclaimed Creative Writing School, an anthology from the Gotham Writers' Workshop (Bloomsbury)

Writing the Breakout Novel, by Donald Maass (Writer's Digest Books)

BOOKS ON MARKETING

A Writer's Time: Making the Time to Write, by Ken Atchity (W.W. Norton)

Aiming at Amazon: The NEW Business of Self Publishing, or How to Publish Your Books with Print on Demand and Online Book Marketing on Amazon.com, by Aaron Shepard (Shepard Publications)

Damn! Why Didn't I Write That? How Ordinary People are Raking in $100,000.00 … or More Writing Nonfiction Books and How You Can Too!, by Marc McCutcheon (Quill Driver Books)

Dan Poynter's Self-Publishing Manual, Vols. 1 and II, by Dan Poynter (Para Publishing)

Get Published! Professionally, Affordably, Fast, by Diane Gedymin and Susan Driscoll (iUniverse)

How to Write a Book Proposal, by Michael Larsen (Writer's Digest Books)

Jeff Herman's Guide to Book Publishers, Editors and Literary Agents, by Jeff Herman (Three Dog Press)

Literary Market Place: The Dictionary of the American Book Publishing Industry, a two-volume set, (Information Today, Inc.)

Magazine Editors Talk to Writers, by Judy Mandell (John Wiley & Sons)
Making the Perfect Pitch: How to Catch a Literary Agent's Eye, by Katherine Sands (The Writer Books)
Print-on-Demand Book Publishing: A New Approach to Printing and Marketing Books for Publishers and Self-Publishing Authors, by Morris Rosenthal (Foner Books)

Red Hot Internet Publicity: An Insider's Guide to Marketing Your Book on the Internet, by Penny C. Sansevieri (Cosimo Books)

The Author's Guide to Bulding an Online Platform: Leveraging the Internet to Sell More Books, by Stephanie Chandler (Quill Driver Books)

The Complete Guide to Book Marketing, by David Cole (Allworth Press)

The Elements of Narrative Nonfiction: How to Write and Sell the Novel of True Events, by Peter Rubie (Quill Driver Books)

The Fast-Track Course on How to Write a Nonfiction Book Proposal, by Stephen Blake Mettee (Quill Driver Books)

The Freelance Success Book: Insider Secrets for Selling Every Word You Write, by David Taylor (Peak Writing Press)

The Portable Writer's Conference: Your Guide to Getting Published, edited by Stephen Blake Mettee (Quill Driver Books)

The Renegade Writer: A Totally Unconventional Guide to Freelance Writing Success, by Linda Formichelli and Diana Burrell (Marion Street Press)

The Well-Fed Writer: Financial Self-Sufficiency as a Freelance Writer in Six Months or Less, by Peter Bowerman (Fanove Publishing)

The Writer's Handbook (issued annually), (The Writer Books)

The Writer's Market (issued annually, with versions for specific genres), (Writer's Digest Books)

Who Does What & Why in Book Publishing, by Clarkson N. Potter (Birch Lane Press)

Write the Perfect Book Proposal: 10 That Sold and Why, by Jeff Herman and Deborah Levine Herman (John Wiley & Sons, Inc.)

SELECTED WRITERS CONFERENCES AND RETREATS

Santa Barbara Writers Conference
sbwriters.com

Bread Loaf Writers' Conference
middlebury.edu/academics/blwc/

Desert Nights, Rising Stars Writers Conference
asu.edu/piper/conference/

Iowa Summer Writing Festival
continuetolearn.uiowa.edu/iswfest/

Jackson Hole Writers Conference
jacksonholewritersconference.com/

MacDowell Colony
macdowellcolony.org/

Sewanee Writers' Conference
sewaneewriters.org/

Squaw Valley Community of Writers
squawvalleywriters.org

The Writers Studio
writerstudio.com/pages/

Tinhouse Summer Writers Workshop
tinhouse.com/workshop/index.htm

Wesleyan Writers Conference
wesleyan.edu/writing/conference/

Yaddo Artists Community
yaddo.org/

WEB SITES FOR WRITERS

Agent Query
agentquery.com/

Alliance of Artists Communities
artistcommunities.org/

American Society of Journalists and Authors
asja.org/index.php

Authorlink
authorlink.com

Bookslut
bookslut.com

EduChoices Best Sites for Writers
educhoices.org/articles/50_of_the_Best_Web sites_for_Writers.html

Fictionaut (Fiction from emerging authors)
fictionaut.com

First Writer (publishers, literary agencies and writing competitions)
firstwriter.com/

Funds for Writers
fundsforwriters.com/

HTMLGiant
htmlgiant.com

McSweeney's Internet Tendency
mcsweeneys.net

National Novel Writing Month
nanowrimo.org/

PEN Center USA
penusa.org/

Poets and Writers magazine
pw.org/

RedRoom (A community of writers)
Redroom.com

Romance Writers of America
rwanational.org/

Science Fiction & Fantasy Writers of America
sfwa.org/

Self-publishing Review
selfpublishingreview.com/

Society of Children's Book Writers and Illustrators
scbwi.org/

The Authors Guild
authorsguild.org/

International Thriller Writers
thrillerwriters.org/

Writers Education (an Authorlink site offering classes and workshops)
writerseducation.com

The Write Thought
TheWriteThought.com

The Writer magazine
writermag.com/

Writer's Digest
writersdigest.com

Writer's Digest's Best 101 Web sites for Writers
writersdigest.com/101BestSites

Marcia Meier is an award-winning journalist, writing coach, and former director of the Santa Barbara Writers Conference.

She has written for numerous publications, including the *Los Angeles Times*, *Santa Barbara Magazine*, *Central Coast Magazine*, *OC Metro* magazine, the *Seattle Times*, and the *Arizona Republic*. She is a contributing writer to *Miller-McCune Magazine* online and an occasional blogger with *The Huffington Post*. Her coffee table book, *Santa Barbara: Paradise on the Pacific*, was published in 1996 by Longstreet Press in Atlanta.

Marcia worked for four daily newspapers in the roles of reporter, copy editor, assistant city editor, and editorial page editor from 1978 until 1995, and she served as editorial page editor of the *Santa Barbara News-Press* for more than six years. She has also taught college-level journalism courses.

Marcia has a degree in journalism and has taught writing privately and for various institutions in Santa Barbara and San Luis Obispo, California. She is a member of the Author's Guild and PEN Center USA.